Grandma Was Right after All!

Grandma was right after all!

PRACTICAL PARENTING WISDOM
FROM THE GOOD OLD DAYS

JOHN ROSEMOND

TYNDALE HOUSE PUBLISHERS, INC.
CAROL STREAM, ILLINOIS

Visit Tyndale online at www.tyndale.com.

TYNDALE and Tyndale's quill logo are registered trademarks of Tyndale House Publishers, Inc.

Grandma Was Right after All!: Practical Parenting Wisdom from the Good Old Days

Copyright © 2015 by John Rosemond. All rights reserved.

Cover and interior illustrations by Mariano Epelbaum. Copyright © by Tyndale House Publishers, Inc. All rights reserved.

Illustration of handbag copyright © 1blackpen/Dollar Photo Club. All rights reserved.

Illustration of speech bubble copyright © ardjo_soekamto/Dollar Photo Club. All rights reserved.

Designed by Ron Kaufmann

Library of Congress Cataloging-in-Publication Data

Rosemond, John K., date.
  Grandma was right after all! : practical parenting wisdom from the good old days / John Rosemond.
    pages cm
    ISBN 978-1-4964-0591-3 (sc)
1. Child rearing.   2. Parenting.   I. Title.
    HQ769.R7134 2015
    649'.1—dc23   2015019769

Printed in the United States of America

21   20   19   18   17   16   15

7   6   5   4   3   2   1

Honor your father and your mother, that your days may be long upon the land which the LORD *your God is giving you.*
—*EXODUS 20:12*

When the foundations are being destroyed, what can the righteous do? —*PSALM 11:3, NIV*

Trust in the LORD *with all your heart, and lean not on your own understanding; in all your ways acknowledge Him, and He shall direct your paths. Do not be wise in your own eyes; fear the* LORD *and depart from evil. It will be health to your flesh, and strength to your bones.* —*PROVERBS 3:5-8*

Understand this, that in the last days there will come times of difficulty. For people will be lovers of self, lovers of money, proud, arrogant, abusive, disobedient to their parents, ungrateful, unholy, heartless, unappeasable, slanderous, without self-control, brutal, not loving good, treacherous, reckless, swollen with conceit, lovers of pleasure rather than lovers of God, having the appearance of godliness, but denying its power. Avoid such people. —*2 TIMOTHY 3:1-5, ESV*

"This is dedicated to the one I love."

(My thanks to Lowman Pauling, Ralph Bass,
The "5" Royales, The Shirelles, The Mamas and
the Papas, and Linda Ronstadt for the inspiration.)

Contents

Introduction

The vernacular or colloquial speech of a culture has meaning beyond the meanings of the words themselves. There is *meaning*—the accepted or dictionary definition of a word—and then there is what is termed *metameaning*—what the words reflect concerning the culture, among other things. Take, for example, the recently popular phrase "Get a life." The words themselves can mean a variety of things, depending on context. The phrase can mean that the person it's spoken to is obsessing about something trivial. Sometimes "Get a life" is used to end a contentious discussion, when the speaker doesn't know what else to say. Whatever the immediate intent or meaning, however, "Get a life" is always, without exception, a sarcastic form of disrespect. It's a dismissal or belittling of another person's point of view, and its recent ubiquity is a reflection of the general deterioration of respect that has taken place in America since the 1960s. "Get a life" is the sort of thing people begin saying to one another when self-centeredness trumps all other social considerations.

In other words, popular vernacular reflects the *zeitgeist*—the culture's mind-set or collective worldview. Likewise, the *loss* of certain vernacular reflects the loss of a certain consensual point of view. When I was growing up, the sayings of Ben Franklin as recorded in his *Poor Richard's Almanack* were still in common usage. Everyone my age, when we were kids, was told, "A penny saved is a penny earned." We also heard "Waste not, want not," another of Franklin's sayings. With a nod to the extremely rare exception, kids don't hear either of those aphorisms anymore. The explanation for their effective disappearance is not that they're old fashioned. Consider that they were still in common use in the 1950s, when they were already two hundred years old—very old fashioned indeed. Ben Franklin's sayings have fallen out of fashion because frugality is no longer a commonly held American virtue. We live in a spendthrift, wasteful age. Consumerism rules the America of today. In fact, a frugal person today is regarded as a cheapskate, a tightwad.

As with sayings like "A penny saved is a penny earned," the entire parenting vernacular of the pre–1960s has virtually disappeared and been replaced by . . . nothing. Well, that's not exactly true. The vernacular of post–1960s American parenting consists of phrases like "Good job!" and "That's terrific!" and "Give me five!" and "You're the best!" and "When you grow up, you can do anything you want to do." This is very new and novel parenting language, for sure. My parents occasionally told me I'd done a good job, but for every "good job," they told me at least three times that I could have done a better job. And when they did tell me I'd done a good job, it didn't carry an exclamation point. It was matter-of-fact, straightforward, and because it was doled out conservatively, I knew I'd really, truly done a good job.

And make no mistake: my parents were typical of their generation. Overwhelmingly my peers tell me their parents were interchangeable with mine. I knew my parents loved me, but they apparently didn't think that being stingy with praise would damage my psyche, and it didn't. Neither did being told that I was acting too big for my britches, which I heard nearly every time I acted too big for my britches.

Taking that example, it is very rare for children today to hear they are acting too big for their britches. Instead, their parents tell them, with great effusion, that they have done a great job—followed by one or more exclamation points—at least once a day (less than that will starve their psyches of warm fuzzies, which are necessary to the proper formation of high self-esteem). Some kids are told they've done a great job or words to that effect at least five times a day. It doesn't matter how well they do something; it's a great job, exclamation point. Give me five! Chest bump! You're the man!

The near extinction of "You're acting too big for your britches" and the rise of the indiscriminate "Great job!" reflect the fact that since the 1950s we have lost one parenting point of view and replaced it with one that is quite the opposite. In the 1950s, modesty was a virtue that parents tried to instill in their kids. Therefore, when children were acting immodestly, they were told they needed to resize themselves to their britches. Today, high self-esteem is the ideal, the brass ring of la dolce vita. Parents in the 1950s and before attempted to rein in their children's natural inclination toward high opinions of themselves. Today's parents, by and large, make no such attempt. They *want* their children to have high opinions of themselves. Supposedly, a high opinion of oneself results in high achievement and good mental health (although the research on both finds exactly the opposite).

The general parenting point of view has changed, and radically so. The point of view that told kids they were busting out of their britches is in history's dustbin, replaced by a point of view that tells kids the lie that everything they do and say is amazing, incredible, awesome, unparalleled in the history of mankind, and that they can do anything they want to do when they grow up.

I am one of those throwbacks who happens to think that the old point of view is more functional and more in children's best interests. The objective evidence is on my side. Kids of the 1950s were a lot more emotionally sturdy than today's kids. That's borne out by reliable statistics. We came to first grade not knowing our ABCs; sat (we were not allowed to get out of our seats when we had finished our classwork) in overcrowded, underfunded classrooms; and had mothers who would not give us much help, if any, with our homework. Worst of all, we could actually fail tests and even entire school years. And yet despite these liabilities we outperformed today's kids at every single grade level. We left home much earlier than today's kids are leaving home, and when we left, we left successfully. (I will note here that there are, of course, exceptions to everything I say about then and now, but my generalities reflect verifiable norms.)

Our physiologies were no different from those of today's kids, nor were we smarter. We were simply raised better. At this point, you can snort if you wish. In these progressive times, it is deemed incorrect to say that the past was better than the present in any regard. That's called "Golden Age" thinking, an attribute, supposedly, of old fogies who just can't accept that times have changed—and changed for the better. Such people (including yours truly, apparently) have a mental disorder that causes them to believe the ridiculous idea that the past, or significant aspects of it, was an improvement over the present.

In response to charges of that sort of "retro-utopian" thinking, let me ask you a couple of questions. First, is it better to be frugal or a spendthrift, to (a) buy only what one needs and can afford or (b) dig a deeper and deeper debt hole with every passing day? Second, is it more socially gracious to (a) be modest about one's accomplishments or (b) trumpet them from the proverbial rooftop? You answered (a) to both questions, did you not? My point is that it is accurate to say that certain aspects—just certain aspects—of the past were, in fact, *better* than their contemporary counterparts. And so it is with my generation. We were raised better, by Tom Brokaw's "Greatest Generation," the generation that overcame every adversity life could throw at them. It's to *their* credit—certainly not ours—that we turned out so well (again, speaking generally but accurately).

It is, however, *our* fault that we Boomers did not realize the gift we'd been given and pass it along to our kids. The pundits convinced us that the parenting baby needed tossing out with the bathwater, that the wheat needed burning with the chaff, that new ideas were better than old ideas, and that the past was a rotten apple and the future a bowl of cherries. And so, in the late 1960s, we came to a fork in the parenting road (to switch metaphors), upon which we followed poet Robert Frost's well-known example and took the road never traveled. And, as Frost observed, that ill-conceived decision sure has made all the difference.

In general, today's parents are experiencing more problems with their kids than their great-grandparents could have *imagined* parents ever experiencing. Their kids talk back to them, ignore them, blatantly disobey them, call them names, and even hit and kick when the parents do not perform satisfactorily. Most of all, their children don't pay attention to them. They don't take them seriously. Today's parents think these problems can be solved by using correct discipline methods (or correct medications). They do not realize that these problems are the inevitable consequences of a faulty point of view, that until their parenting point of view changes for the better—until they begin thinking like parents of the 1950s, in other words—no clever discipline method they use is going to work for long, if it works at all.

So when I'm working with parents who are experiencing

the inevitable consequences of treating children as if they are the most important people not just in the family but who have ever walked the earth, my first approach is to help them change their point of view, to help them begin thinking like their grandparents and great-grandparents. To accomplish that, I often train them in the use of the old parenting vernacular: "You're acting too big for your britches"; "You made this bed, so you're going to lie in it"; "I knew if I gave you a long rope, you'd hang yourself"; "Because I said so"; and so on. The results are often nothing short of amazing. Parents tell me, for example, that within days of first receiving healthy doses of the old parenting language, their kids begin listening, obeying, and acting respectfully. Sometimes this sudden sea change occurs with kids as old as eight or ten who have never before listened to, obeyed, or respected their parents.

After years of hearing these sorts of testimonials, I decided to preserve the old parenting language in a book. My purpose is to help you appreciate and grasp the old parenting point of view—and in so doing, to change your and your children's lives for the better. First, you need to learn the language. The more you talk it, the more you will begin to walk it.

Who Is "Grandma," Anyway?

The Grandma of the title and the numerous references in this book is the typical mother of the pre–psychological parenting age which officially began in 1965 with the publication of psychologist Haim Ginott's groundbreaking bestseller *Between Parent and Child*. As I have explained in other books, most notably *Parent-Babble: How Parents Can Recover from Fifty Years of Bad Expert Advice*, Ginott introduced American parents to a brand-spanking-new set of understandings concerning children and their proper upbringing—understandings based primarily on humanistic psychological theory. It is important to note that these theories, and therefore Ginott's derivative ideas, had never been verified with good research.

Because of his impressive credentials (a PhD psychologist who practiced in the intellectual mecca of Manhattan), parents assumed Ginott knew what he was talking about. In fact, he did not. Like Freud and many other psychologists before and since, Ginott pulled his ideas out of a hat—a very shiny top hat, to be sure, but a hat nonetheless. The amazing success of *Between Parent and Child* set in motion a cascade of parenting books written by psychologists and other mental health professionals, all of which reflected and reinforced the new psychological parenting paradigm. This new paradigm was not Grandma's paradigm, for sure. It was, in fact, as opposite from Grandma's point of view as opposite can be. Most importantly, Grandma's point of view was congruent with a biblical understanding of child and parental responsibilities. That is not to say that every "Grandma" was Bible believing, but even those pre–1960s Grandmas who were unfamiliar with the Bible's teachings concerning children were rearing their children, however unwittingly, according to those teachings. For example, Grandma believed that humility was a virtue. The new psychological paradigm held (and still holds) that high self-esteem is a desirable attribute. Grandma believed spankings had their proper place in the raising of a child. Ginott echoed the rising sentiment of the psychological community when he said that spankings were abusive. There was no agreement whatsoever between Grandma's parenting point of view and methods and the emerging psychological approach.

The Grandma in this book is a mother raising children before 1960. She is, therefore, of my mother's or grandmother's generation. Today, she probably would be a great- or even great-great-grandmother, but the title *Parenting according to Great-Grandma* seemed cumbersome, so for the sake of convenience and clarity, *Grandma* it became.

As the reader will soon discover, Grandma had her feet on solid ground when it came to children. Her eyes were clear, her approach was practical, and perhaps above all else, she was not one to mince words with her kids. Her parenting vernacular, represented by the aphorisms herein (which are not all inclusive, but only the ones she used most often), was—as she would surely have described it—short 'n' sweet.

When people think about historic preservation, they are thinking in terms of buildings, art, books, clothing, and other tangible artifacts of earlier eras. But some of the language of those eras is worth preserving as well. I hope you agree and will do your part.

The Bible Tells Me So!

Honor your father and your mother, that your days may be long upon the land which the LORD *your God is giving you.*

—EXODUS 20:12

I happen to think that the significance of this Scripture verse, also known as the Fifth Commandment, is often under-played. The apostle Paul tells us it is the only commandment that comes "with [a] promise" (Ephesians 6:2), one meaning of which is that through the successful passing of family traditions (which in some cases may also be cultural traditions) from generation to generation, the institution of family is preserved and, therefore, culture is strengthened. One way of honoring one's mother and father is by embracing and preserving the values that were important to them, by passing them on to one's children. When those traditions and associated values are no longer passed along—when parents and ancestors are no longer honored in this fashion—children become prey to relativism, family ties weaken, and culture begins to disintegrate.

This is precisely what happened in the 1960s as America became a postmodern, progressive society. The Baby Boomer generation, taking their cues from the Pied Pipers of Postmodernity, embraced one new, untested idea after another. These new ideas were intentionally antagonistic to the ideas and values that informed previous American generations. In fact, the relativists demonized those ideas and values and told us that we could prevent ourselves from repeating the sins of the past only by jettisoning all the old baggage and replacing it with a brand-new, utopian, post-Christian vision—one that informed every facet of our daily lives.

Replacing the old with the new required that children be raised according to the new point of view, that they be taught the new values from day one. And so, a millennia-old biblical point of view of child and parental responsibilities was replaced with a point of view informed by psychological theory—a mind-set and approach I call postmodern psychological parenting. The consequence of trashing the traditional paradigm has been calamitous for children, parents, marriages, extended families, schools, communities, and culture. For the sake of all concerned, a parenting renewal is desperately needed. The restrengthening of America begins by restoring traditional family values—a "rehonoring" of our foremothers and forefathers. Thus, the book you hold in your hands.

To Ponder and Discuss

What are some specific ways in which you have allowed yourself to be caught up in postmodern psychological parenting? Are you raising your children in a fashion that is far removed from the manner in which your parents raised you (and your grandparents raised them)? If so, what do you think would be different about your children's behavior and attitudes if you had "honored your father and your mother" and followed their example when it came to your own kids? Were you easier to discipline than your kids are? Why? What is it that your parents did that made their parenting experience so much less fraught with stress?

1

"Because I Said So"

It's safe to say that the parenting aphorism most associated with the good old days—when children respected adults and adults did not try to be liked by children—is "Because I said so." Sometimes those four words ended with an exclamation point, sometimes they ended with an added "that's why," and sometimes they ended with both.

I heard those four words fairly often when I was a child. So did every other child who grew up in the 1950s. At least, I've yet to meet someone my age who claims to have had parents who did not say these words (although I'm reasonably certain a few someones of the sort do exist). The exchange between parent and child might have gone something like this:

Child: May I have a bowl of ice cream?

Mother: No, you may not.

Child: Why not?

Mother: Because I said so, that's why not.

Child: But why?

Mother: Goats butt.

Child: What does that mean?

Mother: It means you're not having ice cream.

Or the exchange might have involved something a parent told a child to do, as in the following example:

Mother: It's time for you to pick up your toys and put them away.

Child: But why?

Mother: Because I said so.

Child: Ugh! That's not a reason!

Mother: Well, it's the only one you're getting, unless you want me to give your backside a reason.

It is important to note that in both of these examples, the child demands to know the reason behind his mother's decision or instruction precisely because she does *not* give a reason—she does *not* explain herself. In the first example, the mother does not say, "No, honey, I'm so sorry, but you can't have ice cream right now because it's too close to dinner." In the second example, the mother does not say, "Sweetie pie, I need to run the vacuum cleaner in here, so I need you to pick up your toys and put them away." The very absence of a reason forces the child to demand (it is not, after all, a polite request) a reason, to demand to know why or why not. In other words, for a parent to say "Because I said so" requires that the parent *not* explain his or her decisions and instructions.

Unlike parents back in the golden age of child rearing (it was not called *parenting* back then), today's parents explain themselves. They give their children reasons for the decisions they make and the instructions they convey. And because they explain themselves, they end up having arguments with their children.

In the above ice-cream example, had the mother given a reason for her decision—if she had told her child that he could not have ice cream because dinner was imminent—her child would very likely have come back with "No it's not! I'll still eat my dinner! I promise!" The mother then would have engaged the child in debate, trying to get the child to agree with her that he should not have ice cream when dinner is right around the proverbial corner.

This mother's fantasy child eventually says, "You know, Mom, you're absolutely right. When you explain it like that, I can't help but agree. I mean, any intelligent person would have to agree, and you have that sticker on the back window of your minivan that says I'm in the honors program at school, so yes, because you've made a rational appeal to my outstanding intelligence, I agree that it's not a good idea for me to have ice cream right now. Mom, I love you for many reasons, not the least of which is that you take such care to make sure I eat a balanced diet. Thank you, Mom."

And had the second mother told her child that she wanted him to pick up his toys so she could vacuum, he would very likely have come back with something like "I'm playing! Why do you have to vacuum now? Why can't you wait?"

The mother would then attempt to get the child to agree that vacuuming takes precedence over playing and that due to her many other responsibilities, this is the best time for her to vacuum, and therefore he should happily pick up his toys and put them away.

That mother's fantasy child says, "Say no more, Mom. You've convinced me. I now realize that adult responsibilities are more important than a child's play. That realization is something I will cherish forever, Mom, as I cherish you, and you can believe I am going to do all I can to pass that lesson to my kids. Thank you, Mom."

If the fantasy responses from these two fantasy children sound fantastic to the point of absurdity, it's because they are. No child anywhere or in any historical time has ever said anything along those lines to a parent. Granted, some children, as adults, come back to their parents and thank them for raising them so well. Both of my kids did that in their early twenties. But it took them becoming adults to understand and appreciate an adult point of view.

Reasons, Schmeasons

Today's parents believe that children deserve reasons. That is, after all, what the parenting experts have been telling parents since the 1960s. And so, today's parents explain themselves to their children—they give reasons. And so, their children argue. It's a fundamental cause-and-effect relationship: explanations cause arguments. My point is that arguments between parent and child occur not because children have some "argumentative gene" or "argumentative biochemical" in their bodies or because the part of the brain that governs respectful obedience is yet underdeveloped, but simply because parents give reasons and explanations. Those reasons and explanations stimulate pushback in the form of children telling parents that their reasons and explanations don't wash, that they aren't good enough. At that point, parents begin defending their reasons and explanations; thus, arguments between parents and children abound.

To summarize: in the absence of reasons and explanations, children have nothing to push back against; thus, no arguments between parents and children. Simple, isn't it?

A woman once told me she had a pronounced negative reaction to the thought of saying "Because I said so" because her parents had often screamed those four words at her with an implied threat of soon-to-come violence. I had to agree that her parents had misused the "Because I said so" privilege. But her parents' mistake does not mean those four words are invalid. It should go without saying that "Because I said so" should not be screamed at a child or said in a threatening tone of voice, but then that applies to anything parents say. In other words, simply because some parents wrap those four words in a rigid, unreasonable, threatening attitude, they are not, in and of themselves, rigid, unreasonable, and threatening. My thesaurus gives the following synonyms for *reasonable*: sensible, rational, logical, and practical. And indeed, "Because I said so" is all of that.

First, it is the truth. The parent has made a decision. The parent has conveyed the decision—"you cannot," "I will not," or "you will"—to the child. Therefore, at the most basic of levels, "Because I said so" is simply a statement of fact.

Second, "Because I said so" stops the potential for argument dead in its deadly tracks. As I said above, when a parent refuses to explain, the child has nothing with which to manufacture an argument. The child's inclination to argue hits a stone wall. This is good, because when parents and children argue, no one profits.

Third, "Because I said so" reflects a ubiquitous social reality: to wit, people in positions of authority are not required to explain themselves to the people over whom they have authority. This applies to military officers, teachers, college professors, workplace managers, and business owners. Children who enter adulthood already having accepted that social reality—having become accustomed to it courtesy of their parents—hold a distinct advantage over the children who enter adulthood believing—again, courtesy of their parents—that they deserve reasons and explanations whenever they are given an instruction or are informed of a rule or a boundary.

It is a reality that even in a democratic society, authority figures frequently make arbitrary decisions. A boss decides things are going to be done this way rather than that way; that the line is going to be drawn in one place rather than another; that the standard will be based on this measure as opposed to that one; and so on. Why? Because the boss says so, that's why. That is a boss's prerogative. And that's that, until the boss changes his or her mind or a new boss comes along.

A prime example of what I'm saying just occurred to me because I happen to be writing this chapter on April 15— Tax Day. On this date I pay to the government a certain percentage of my income. I do not determine said percentage; the government does. Furthermore, I do not pay income tax because I think the United States government deserves the money. In fact, the government has consistently failed to demonstrate good stewardship of my hard-earned money. In my estimation (and the estimation of many), the United States government is fiscally irresponsible. If a business was run the way our elected representatives run the country, the business would go belly up in less than six months.

I do not want to pay what the Internal Revenue Service says I owe. No government official has ever given me a good reason why I should pay what I pay. Yet I pay it nonetheless. Why? Because "they" say so. Period. End of story.

Likewise, about four of every five parental decisions are founded on nothing more substantial than arbitrary personal predilection. The Wilsons do not allow their kids to have non-organic food; the Smiths do. Both sets of kids are healthy, well behaved, and do well in school. Therefore, the Wilsons cannot defend their prohibition by pointing to some better outcome. Nonetheless, it is legitimate for them to deny their children food that is not certified organic. And when their children ask why they are denied foods the Smith kids enjoy, the most honest answer Mr. and Mrs. Wilson can give is "Because we say so."

Not only do today's parents feel obligated to explain themselves to their children, they also seem to believe that their explanations must satisfy and pacify the children in question. Consequently, those explanations take on a persuasive, pleading, even apologetic, character. Implicit in this is the absolutely absurd idea that parents don't have a right to enforce a decision unless (a) it can be supported by reasons other than personal preference, (b) the children understand those reasons, and (c) the children agree with them. This perspective causes lots of unnecessary pain for both parents and kids.

Now, hear me clearly. I'm not saying that parents should never give reasons to children; I'm saying that parents should make no attempt to reason with children, and there is a big difference between the two. Reasoning is the futile attempt to persuade your children that your point of view is valid. Let's face it: your children will understand your point of view when they themselves are parents and no sooner. If you want to explain yourself, then by all means do so. But don't expect your children to agree. When they don't, simply say, "I'm not asking you to agree. If I were you, I wouldn't agree with me either. You have my permission to disagree, but you don't have my permission to disobey." In other words, children do what they are told, not because their parents succeed at providing an explanation that smooths their ruffled feathers, but simply because they've been told. So even in the act of giving reasons, the bottom line is still "Because I said so."

The Bible Tells Me So!

Children, obey your parents in the Lord, for this is right. —EPHESIANS 6:1

Children, obey your parents in everything, for this pleases the Lord.
—COLOSSIANS 3:20, NIV

One Sunday when Willie and I were visiting a church in the mountains of North Carolina, the pastor happened to be preaching on parenting. It quickly became obvious that he had been greatly influenced by psychological theory because his sermon could have been taken right out of my college child development textbook. He was talking about how important it is for parents to help their kids develop high self-esteem and how children need lots of attention and praise. Toward the end of his sermon, he said, "I don't think it's right for a parent to say, 'Because I said so.'" Willie and I looked at each other with raised eyebrows. Had this pastor never read Ephesians 6:1 or

Colossians 3:20? Those passages simply instruct children to obey, and the only reason given is *because a child's obedience is pleasing to God.*

A parent's authority is assigned by God. As such, a parent is called to reflect God's unconditional love and unequivocal authority. It is a sufficient reason for us to obey God because he is the one holy and almighty God—because he says so. That is, therefore, a sufficient reason why a child should obey his or her parents (assuming that they honor God in their parenting). Note that Paul does not say that children should obey their parents because their parents provide good reasons. Rather, children should obey "in everything" simply because that's the way God wants it. Children who experience the joy of obedience to their parents are taking a huge first step toward experiencing the joy of obedience to God.

To Ponder and Discuss

Do you often feel obligated to give your children "good" reasons for the decisions you make and the instructions you give them? If so, can you identify the social and cultural factors that have caused you to try to reason with your kids? Do you find yourself engaging in frequent unproductive arguments with your kids? Are you ready to reclaim your authority and stop arguing with children who are only satisfied when they win?

2
"Children Should Be Seen and Not Heard"

I often conduct polls with my audiences, one of which illuminates the extent to which people believe that today's parenting is a great improvement over the old-fashioned stuff. I'll be standing in front of an audience of, say, five hundred folks, and I'll say, "Raise your hand if you believe that children should be seen and not heard." Maybe twenty-five hands go up, most of which belong to people who, at a glance, look to be my age or thereabouts.

"Okay," I say, "now, raise your hand again if you believe that when children are in a room otherwise occupied by adults who are having a conversation, it is right and proper for the children to pay attention to what is being said and to not do anything to attract attention to themselves." Five hundred hands go up.

Isn't that fascinating? All I did, of course, was say the same thing twice—the first time I used the pre–1960s expression; the second time I translated it for the benefit of today's parents. The exercise illustrates the success of professional propaganda in causing modern parents to believe that pre–1960s parenting harmed children's psyches and should be disdained. This, of course, is not true in the least. Back then, child mental health was considerably better than it is today. School achievement and classroom behavior were much better as well. And it is a fact that back then children were told, on occasion, that if they wanted to listen to an adult conversation, they had to be "seen and not heard."

This put children in their proper role: student. It defined the adults as older, wiser, and more knowledgeable—people from whom the children, if they listened keenly to the conversation, and even if they did not understand all that was said, might learn something. As such, telling children that they were to be seen and not heard *benefited* them. Granted, it benefited the adults as well because if the children consented to being seen and not heard, the adults would be able to carry on an uninterrupted conversation. But the primary benefit accrued to the children.

I myself benefited on more than a few occasions. My mother and stepfather were very well-educated people who had a number of equally well-educated friends—physicians, scientists, college professors, and the like. There were many times when my parents took me along to dinner parties at their friends' homes (during the meal, we children sat at a separate table, much to our delight). On the way, my stepfather would remind me that when adults were talking, I was to be seen and not heard. That was fine with me. After dinner, the other kids (who had also been told to be seen and not heard) and I would sit in the room with the adults and listen while they talked about highly erudite things like the latest research into cell-wall porosity or the relative merits of Mozart versus Beethoven. (No, I'm not kidding.)

On the way home from these gatherings, where I felt like I'd been admitted to a meeting of superior beings, I'd ask my parents questions like "What is a double helix?" And they would attempt to explain emerging DNA science in language a child my age could understand. My continuing love of science and high-minded questions concerning life's origins—and make no mistake, I am convinced beyond any doubt that all the objective scientific evidence confirms the Genesis account of Creation—started in those living rooms, listening as adults held high-minded conversations, being seen and not heard.

It goes without saying that if I had been allowed to interject my impulsive thoughts into these conversations, I would not have learned nearly as much. I would have sidetracked these fascinating conversations. People would have felt the need to explain things to me, and because it is the nature of children, the more attention I received from these interruptions, the more I would have interrupted and the less I would have learned.

Was there a kinder, gentler way of telling me that I was to listen and not talk? Yes. My parents could have said, "Now, after dinner the adults are going to gather in the living room and talk, and you may sit in the room and listen to us, but you are not to interrupt us. If you listen, you will learn something. Sound good?"

Is that kinder and gentler? I suppose so. But that raises the question, Would it have been more effective? Not a chance. "You are to be seen and not heard" was much more straightforward, and as such it sounded far more authoritative. The kinder, gentler alternative sounds *persuasive*, as though the parents are *asking* children to please consider their request. In other words, children who are given the kinder, gentler version are more likely to interrupt. Children are much more likely to obey when instructions sound authoritative, as if the adults mean business, than when instructions sound persuasive. I did not interrupt these adult conversations because the expectation was stated concisely and authoritatively. It was clear to me that my parents were not making a request or a suggestion for me to take up with my internal committee of one.

Relationships Need Borders Too!

In a larger sense, "Children should be seen and not heard" also refers to the fact that in those days, a boundary existed between adult society and child society. Adults were adults, and children were children, and the twain did not intermingle much at all. Furthermore, everyone understood—children included—that adults were superior to children. For these reasons, children looked up to adults. Adults belonged to an exclusive society that we children wanted someday to become members of. This society had its own language, its own jokes, and lots of subtleties, none of which we children understood. An adult would say something, and then there would be a moment of silence, and then everyone would laugh. What was so funny? And if one of us had the temerity to ask, "Why did everyone laugh?" an adult would smile and say, "Little pitchers have big ears." And everyone would laugh again.

Boundaries are important to the functionality of relationships. The primary purpose of the adult-child relationship is to ensure that children receive the love they need to become compassionate and the leadership they need to become responsible. Compassion and responsibility make people good neighbors and good citizens. So by raising children properly, parents strengthen community bonds and strengthen America through the next generation.

These purposes require that children pay attention to adults; that they look up, literally and figuratively, to adults. Looking up to adults causes children to aspire to become adults themselves. That requires a boundary between adults and children, a boundary that distinguishes adults as superior beings. The boundary in question also separates adults and children into two mostly separate worlds that overlap at times but are distinct most of the time. Simply put, children need to know that they are children (knowledge that gives them freedom to fully enjoy their childhoods), and adults need to act like adults.

This is a fact: children are not going to look up to adults who act like they want to be, or want the approval of, children. Unfortunately, many adults today act like they want to be perceived by children as "cool." To accomplish this silly goal, they eradicate any boundary between themselves and the children whose approval they seek. In so doing, they diminish themselves in the eyes of those kids. Those children would probably say they "like" those adults, but they do not truly respect them.

When my daughter Amy was in high school, she began having a conflict with her drama teacher. He was young and wanted to be liked by his students. According to Amy, he had favorites, and she was not one of them. As is my inclination, I gave this teacher the benefit of the doubt but kept a close eye on the situation. One day the teacher called, and I answered the phone. He launched into a series of complaints about Amy. I listened, and when he had finished, I told him that although I would always support his authority, I had the distinct impression that he was his own worst enemy. I shared with him my feeling that he was trying to be popular with certain students and was losing the respect of all of them as a consequence. He didn't seem to want to talk further, so the conversation ended.

Many years later, I met him at a social gathering, and he reminded me of the time we had talked on the phone. He told me that although I'd stung his pride, I also caused him to think long and hard about his responsibilities. "You were absolutely right," he said. "That conversation caused me to be a much better teacher."

As that story illustrates, boundaries are essential to facilitating mutual respect in a relationship. A woman who does not establish a boundary in relationships with men, for example, is not going to be respected by them. They may enjoy her company (under certain circumstances), but respect is out of the question. Those men will definitely take advantage of her. Likewise, adults who do not establish boundaries between themselves and children are not going to be respected by those kids. Again, the kids may *like* those adults, but respect is not synonymous with being liked. Those kids will try to manipulate the adults and take advantage of them, and they definitely will take the adults for granted.

I'll say it again: regardless of the nature of a relationship, a boundary is essential to respect. In the employer-employee relationship, it is up to the employer to establish and maintain the boundary. In the teacher-student relationship, it is up to the teacher to establish and maintain the boundary. And in the adult-child relationship, including the parent-child relationship, it is up to the adult to establish and maintain the boundary. That does not mean that adults and children cannot intermingle at times, have fun together, talk, or cuddle. It simply means that the intermingling, having fun, talking, or cuddling takes place within the context of the unspoken understanding that adults are not the children's buddies; that they are first and foremost authority figures. If that understanding exists, the intermingling will be more satisfying to both parties anyway.

It is a good thing for children to look up to and respect adults. That's also a good thing for adults, but the most good accrues to the children. When children aspire to become adults, they grow up faster. Because they are trying to gain the approval of adults, they become more competent more quickly. They pay better attention to teachers and other adults. They are more obedient, and the research is clear (and common sense confirms) that obedient children are much happier than disobedient children. Finally, appropriate adult-child boundaries promote early, successful emancipation.

Appropriate boundaries between adults and children include sleeping in different beds, having access to different media, enjoying different amounts of freedom and different standards of living, and children being seen and not heard when adults are engaged in adult conversation.

The Bible Tells Me So!

The fear of the LORD is the beginning of knowledge, but fools despise wisdom and instruction. —PROVERBS 1:7

The fear of the LORD is the beginning of wisdom, and the knowledge of the Holy One is understanding. —PROVERBS 9:10

Train up a child in the way he should go, and when he is old he will not depart from it. —*PROVERBS 22:6*

The fear of the LORD is the beginning of wisdom. —*PSALM 111:10*

Discipline is often thought of rather simplistically—as the process by which a parent corrects misbehavior. Indeed, correction is one important aspect of discipline, but setting boundaries is equally important to the overall purpose. Boundaries serve several functions: they protect children from possible physical harm, keep them out of trouble, and create important distinctions between people. Concerning the latter, the most important interpersonal distinction that parents need to communicate to their children is the difference—the dividing line if you will—between adults and children. This is absolutely necessary to defining children as disciples and parents and other adults as authority figures.

An appropriate boundary in the parent-child relationship serves as a model for children's relationships to other adults. That boundary causes children to "look up," both literally and figuratively. It is essential for causing children to respect their parents, respect that is then transferred to other adults whom the children's parents define as authority figures. It is unhealthy for children to fail to understand that they are not members of adult society. That understanding guarantees them a valid childhood; therefore, the lack of that boundary denies them a valid childhood.

A clearly defined adult-child boundary—which, again, begins with parents who communicate to their children that they are not their peers and certainly not members of their marriage—confers a separate, distinct identity upon children. As such, it greatly clarifies for them how the interpersonal world is organized and works. When boundaries operate properly, each person has a clear role comprised of unique responsibilities and privileges.

The question then becomes, Is there a biblical basis for establishing boundaries in the parent-child relationship? The answer is an unequivocal yes. Proverbs 22:6 is perhaps the most well known of all Scriptures concerning parents and children. It tells parents to "train" their children in keeping with the adults they want them to become. This refers to a clear distinction between trainer and trainee, parent and child. Without such a distinction, children would have no reason to accept training from their parents.

Bible passages that describe the benefits of fearing the Lord refer to the ultimate parent-child relationship. The word "fear" refers to awestruck reverence, not shaking in one's boots (although there may be times when such trembling is appropriate). I need not, I trust, point out the nature or extent of the boundary between God and man. I will only point out that ultimate respect for the ultimate Parent requires an ultimate boundary (which has been breached once, solely for mankind's benefit, and said breach did not weaken the ultimate nature of said boundary at all).

To Ponder and Discuss

Do your children seem to think they are your peers, that whatever privileges you enjoy, they should enjoy as well? Do your children lack appropriate respect for you? If so, does this lack extend to other adults? Could you do a better job of describing and enforcing a boundary between you and your kids? How?

3

"You Made This Bed, and Now You're Going to Have to Lie in It"

"You made this bed, and now you're going to have to lie in it" were some of the most dreaded words to come out of my parents' mouths. I'd just done something wrong, and I'd been caught, and I was in big trouble, and I was going to be punished, and I came to my parents and told them what I'd done and asked them to help me by stepping in on my behalf and talking to the adult I was in trouble with—a teacher, perhaps—and trying to persuade him or her to lighten up. And my parents would look at each other and turn back to me, and one of them would say what I least wanted to hear.

In other words, I was going to have to accept the consequences of what I had done. I had made a choice, and now

I was going to experience the result of having made that choice. But more than that, "You made this bed . . ." also meant that no one else was going to lie in that very uncomfortable bed with me. My parents certainly were not going to. They were not going to intervene in any way. They were not going to speak on my behalf, defend me, or come to my assistance in any other way, shape, or form. I was on my own, and believe me, the bed in question was the loneliest bed in the whole wide world.

Here's a true story to illustrate the point. I became a major behavior problem in the seventh grade. I disrupted the class with inappropriate comments and other stupidities. Other kids (the boys, mostly) laughed at my shenanigans, so I kept them up. These days I'd be tested, diagnosed, and medicated. Back then I was simply punished. My parents, teachers, and the principal punished me over and over again but to no avail. I was immune—or so I thought. I was a straight-A student, after all. What could they do to me? Keep me after school? Make me write sentences? So what? They had no power over me. I was too smart for them, as evidenced by my invention of the Amazing Multi-Writer—five pens held together with rubber bands and tongue depressors—which enabled me to write five sentences simultaneously.

One February afternoon, my parents went to my school for what I thought was a routine report-card conference. They were gone longer than expected. When they came home, they sat me down, and my stepfather said, "I'm going to say this once and once only. If you are reprimanded by a teacher for any reason between now and the end of the school year, you are going to repeat the seventh grade next year."

They both got up and walked out of the room as I sat there with my mouth hanging wide open. I got up and ran after them. "But what if the teacher who reprimands me is wrong?" I asked, panic stricken. "What if I really didn't do it? What if it was someone else?"

My stepfather said, "I've said all I'm going to say." And then they continued walking away.

The next day I demonstrated to my teachers how wrong they had been about me. I wasn't a behavior problem! Look! I was the best-behaved kid in the class! For the rest of that academic year, I never spoke out of turn; I completed all my work on time and then asked for extra work; I never laughed at someone else's joke; I faced forward only; and when a teacher called on me, I gave serious rather than sarcastic answers. My behavior disorder was cured in one day by two parents who made me lie in the very uncomfortable bed I had made.

The notion that children should, for their own good, lie in the beds they make—that they should take full, unmitigated responsibility for their actions—has become nearly extinct.

Who lies in the beds children make today? Parents, that's who! Today, children do something bad or fail to do something they should have done, and their *parents* end up feeling bad about it. It's axiomatic that the person who feels bad about the problem is the person who is going to do whatever it takes to solve it. And sure enough, today's parents can be counted on to solve problems their children create whether through irresponsibility, malice, or just plain foolishness. And quite often the parents of whom I speak "solve" the problems by denying they exist or shifting the blame.

A good example of this involves problems children create at school by either misbehaving or not doing the work they're supposed to do. When I was a kid and children were expected to lie in the beds they made, if children created problems at school, (a) they were punished at school, then (b) the teacher called home and informed their parents what had happened, and they were punished again at home. This very psychologically incorrect double whammy usually prevented recurrences of the problem in question.

Today, children create problems at school and (a) they are not punished at school because schools have reason to fear lawsuits brought by parents who believe their kids are being treated unjustly by dastardly, vindictive, heartless people who became teachers in order to treat children with malice on a daily basis, and (b) if teachers have the guts and gall to call the children's parents to report the problems, whatever they are, the parents are likely to defend their children. (I'm not talking about all parents, of course, but enough that they deserve special mention.) They actually deny that what thirty- or forty- or fifty-year-old professionals—who have dedicated their lives to the betterment of the lives of children—are telling them is the truth. No, the teachers are lying, and the seven-year-old children are telling the truth.

The parents know their children are telling the truth because "they have never lied to us." That's what many of these parents say. So guess what? Teachers end up suffering for what children have done. Children make the beds, and teachers are ultimately forced—often by administrators who just want to keep peace—to lie in them.

The list goes on: A six-year-old bites another child in school, and the biter's parents claim that the fault belongs to the bitten child. He "asked for it" by annoying their six-year-old. A ten-year-old girl sends another girl an inappropriate text message, and her parents respond to the other parents' complaint by telling them that their daughter is immature and shouldn't have a cell phone anyway. A sixteen-year-old is arrested for driving under the influence, and his parents hire the best lawyer in town to defend him. (Those are real-life examples, by the way.)

What are the benefits of children lying in the beds they make, of having no parental buffer between their actions and the consequences of those actions? The most immediate benefit of having to accept full responsibility for misbehavior is no longer misbehaving. Lying on a bed of nails that they have made for themselves is the best guarantee that children will never repeat whatever resulted in them having to lie on a bed of nails.

And make no mistake, as I continue to say at every possible opportunity, misbehavior is an impediment to personal satisfaction, otherwise known as happiness. The most obedient kids are also the best-adjusted kids. And be assured, having obedient children is not an accident, a random genetic event. It is the result of parents who insist upon obedience and hold children completely responsible for their every action.

Last but not least, children who lie in the beds they make are going to be prepared for successful emancipation at an earlier age than would otherwise be the case. The average age at which males attain complete economic independence has increased from twenty-one in 1970 to nearly twenty-eight by 2010. I'm convinced that this dramatic increase is largely the result of failing to hold children completely responsible for their behavior and of parents who run perpetual interference for their kids.

To summarize, the benefits of children having to lie in the beds they make are good behavior, happiness, and earlier emancipation. What more could children want? Or their parents, for that matter?

The Bible Tells Me So!

Do not be deceived, God is not mocked; for whatever a man sows, that he will also reap.
—*GALATIANS 6:7*

Throughout the Old Testament, we read that on one occasion after another, God made the Israelites lie in beds they had made for themselves. They paid for their idol worship during the Exodus by having to wander in the Sinai Desert for forty years, for example. They paid again for their apostasies by being defeated in war and taken to Babylon. Like children, God's chosen people were slow learners.

Sooner or later, bad things happen to people who do bad things. That principle is as much a part of God's design as the speed of light or the laws of thermodynamics. It is vital to children's proper socialization, not to mention a right understanding of their proper relationship and responsibilities to God, that they come to grips with that fundamental principle.

To Ponder and Discuss

Do you regularly allow your children to lie in the beds they have made? If not, why not? Are you reluctant to do anything that would cause your children to be upset with you? When you do something that causes them to be upset, do you feel that you may have done the wrong thing? What can you do today to begin allowing them to lie in beds they make?

4

"You Are a Little Fish in a Big Pond"

If I heard it once, I heard it a hundred times. "No matter how much you accomplish in this world, John Rosemond," one of my parents would lecture, "you would do well to always remember that you are really just a little fish in a big pond."

I always felt like saying, "No! I'm not going to be a little fish! I've got dreams! I'm going to be a Big Fish!" But I didn't. I just stood there and looked at them, wondering why they felt the need to keep saying this to me. I now realize they kept saying it to me because they knew I wanted to be a Big Fish. In fact, by the time I was in the seventh grade, I already thought I was one (see my story in chapter 3).

So here I am, fifty or so years later, and in many people's

eyes, I am a Big Fish. I'm a nationally (even internationally) known parenting expert. I've written twenty books, many of which are bestsellers in the parenting field. My syndicated newspaper column appears weekly in about two hundred newspapers. I am one of the most in-demand public speakers in my field. People frequently recognize me in restaurants, in malls, in airports and on airplanes, and on the street. I'm a Big Fish, right?

One of my favorite musicians is Doug Sahm, whose original group, The Sir Douglas Quintet, was famous for the hit "She's about a Mover." Sahm's music blended lots of American roots influences into a unique sound. He titled one of his songs "You Never Get Too Big and You Sure Don't Get Too Heavy That You Don't Have to Stop and Pay Some Dues Sometime." It's got to be the longest song title of all time. In the 1980s, when I realized that I was becoming fairly well known for my iconoclastic parenting advice, I thought of that song, and I've kept it in mind ever since. That, along with my parents' repetitious reminders to the effect that I'm a small fish, has kept me from becoming too big for my britches, from thinking the world revolves around me, from thinking of myself as a Big Fish.

I've had the opportunity to meet people who obviously think they are Big Fish. I once realized, for example, that I was sitting less than five feet from one of the most famous basketball players in history. The word *legendary* applies. We were waiting for the same airplane. I said, "Excuse me, but my son is a huge fan of yours. Would you be willing to autograph this piece of paper to Eric? He'd be thrilled beyond belief." Big Fish looked at me with complete disdain and went back to reading his newspaper. I think that meant no. (I bumped into a famous country-music singer in an airport once and asked him to sign a piece of paper to my secretary, who was a big fan of his. He smiled, signed, and wished me a blessed day. I instantly became a fan as well.)

Then there was the time I met a Major Political Figure and his wife in the dining area of a bed-and-breakfast in New York. We were speaking at the same conference. During my standing, face-to-face conversation with MPF, his wife suddenly wedged her body between mine and his, her back to me, and began speaking to him as if I weren't there. Then, without so much as a "Nice to meet you," they left the building. (I won't identify her other than to say she has since become a leading figure in American politics.)

Then there was the guy I shared the green room with as we were waiting for our respective turns on *The View*. You'd know his name, for sure—a famous American actor, spokesperson for a major cause, and all that la-di-da. There we were in the waiting room, just two average, ordinary guys (or so I thought). I tried to strike up a conversation along the lines of "Did you fly in from Los Angeles?" Without looking up from the magazine he was reading (might have been an article about himself), he mumbled something that sounded vaguely like yes. *Maybe I could bond with him*, I thought, *if I let him know I've watched his films.* So I said, "I thought you were very good in (his latest movie)." Mumble. Okay, he got his point across. I was not worth talking to. I was a nobody. The Almighty Him, on the other hand, was a Somebody, a Big Fish, and Big Fish was not going to stoop to give Johnny "Little Fish" Rosemond the time of day.

When you meet a person who actually believes he or she is a Big Fish, it's almost startling. If they don't manage to make you feel like slime, you realize they have a major, pronounced character defect. They refuse to accept the truth about themselves: that no matter what they've accomplished, no matter how many people know their names, no matter how many people think they're wonderful, they are really just little fish in a big pond. Or, as Doug Sahm put it, "You never get too big and you sure don't get too heavy that you don't have to stop and pay some dues sometime."

Their parents must have never told them what my parents told me about little fish in big ponds. That's too bad, because I know only too well that coming to grips with the fact that you're a little fish is what keeps your feet on solid ground and your head out of the intoxicating clouds of perpetual self-delusion. The paradox is that little fish do *big* things. They pay attention to other people, for starters. They look for opportunities to do things for other people. They try to help other people feel comfortable. They try to make other people feel like they're worth something.

Children need to learn early on that being a little fish is the way one thanks God for the gift of human life. You thank God for the gift of human life by treating other human beings (with whom you share that gift) with respect, kindness, compassion, charity, and care. God loves you, and you thank God for his inestimable love by sharing it with others.

The problem is that children are inclined toward wanting to think of themselves as Big Fish. That's what toddler tantrums are all about. Their legendary rages occur because they believe they deserve to have what they want, and their parents are obligated, therefore, to give it to them on demand. At least 95 percent of toddler tantrums have nothing to do with need or pain. They are all about *want*. Toddlers possess a selfish nature and want the people in their world to feed it constantly. Their selfish nature decides it wants something, and that's that. If the adults in question do not give it to them, they go into a rage. Toddlers' selfish nature is the Big Fish. Their parents' job is to teach them that they're really little fish—that being little fish is the only valid way to live. That's a tough job, because it requires that their parents face directly into the hurricane and refuse to budge. If they can manage to do that, the hurricane will burn itself out by the time the children are around three years old. If the parents budge—by giving in to the tantrums or throwing tantrums of their own (the hurricane succeeds in moving them, in other words)—then the hurricane gets stronger, and they will have more and more difficulty standing up to it.

This is done for the children's sake, not the parents'. It goes without saying that children who do not throw tantrums are a lot happier than children who do. Children who accept "no" are a lot happier than children who believe they can change "no" to "yes" by turning themselves into Category

5 hurricanes. Likewise, children who come to grips with the fact that they're little fish in a big pond are a lot happier than children who are allowed to continue thinking they're Big Fish.

The three real-life Big Fish I described above: Do you think they're happy campers? Of course not! They may have money, they may enjoy (if that's the proper word) celebrity status, but they are not happy campers. How do I know? Because people can only be truly happy (meaning they are, first, completely satisfied with their lives, and second, that their satisfaction is not tied to material things or prestige) if they take my parents' words to heart and realize that no matter how much they accomplish in this world, they are really just little fish in a big pond.

Thank you, Mom and Dad, for teaching me one of the most valuable lessons of all. Would that all parents would do the same. Maybe then the six o'clock news would be about happy stuff.

The Bible Tells Me So!

Do nothing from selfish ambition or conceit, but in humility count others more significant than yourselves. Let each of you look not only to his own interests, but also to the interests of others. Have this mind among yourselves, which is yours in Christ Jesus, who, though he was in the form of God, did not count equality with God a thing to be grasped,

but emptied himself, by taking the form of a servant, being born in the likeness of men. —PHILIPPIANS 2:3-7, ESV

If the first thing everyone in the world—rich, poor, famous, ordinary, workers, owners, rulers, the ruled—did upon waking up every morning was read Philippians 2:3-11, think of how much better life on this earth would be! We have the opportunity to obtain eternal life because God made himself into a little fish—"made himself nothing," as Paul puts it. What a concept! Children need to learn that we honor what Jesus did for all of us by taking on his character in our dealings with others. Children need to learn that the purpose of life is to serve, not to be served (see Matthew 20:28). Their lives depend on it.

To Ponder and Discuss

Do your kids sometimes act like they think they're Big Fish? Can you identify ways in which you may have fostered that belief? What are some ways you can help your kids grasp the fact that God wants little fish?

5
"I Knew If I Gave You Enough Rope, You'd Hang Yourself"

In my senior year of high school, I wanted more than anything else to qualify as cool, with-it, groovy, fab, and other dated adjectives of the sort. I'd been a nerdy four-eyes for too long. However, there was a slight problem. The kids who occupied the top tier of the popularity pyramid had made it perfectly clear I didn't measure up. By default, I fell in with a group of four guys who skirted the edges of delinquency. To my knowledge, none of them had ever been arrested, but that was soon to change.

One of them—his name was Terry—received a 1965 Pontiac GTO from his parents for graduation. Back then, this was the car of every high-school boy's dreams. That summer, the five of us spent long hours cruising in Terry's *très* cool ride. We were looking for girls, of course, although how we thought we were going to fit anyone else in the car is beyond me.

One gorgeous summer day we were driving around a residential neighborhood that lay within the feeder zone for our high school when a car full of guys passed us going in the other direction. We recognized them as students from a rival high school. How outrageous! They were looking for girls in our territory! We quickly swung around the block and passed them again. This time we yelled various slurs at them, mostly impugning their parentage. Sure enough, they yelled various equally impugning slurs back at us. Both cars drove around the block again and stopped, facing one another, at the intersection of two normally quiet suburban lanes. The cars emptied, and what ensued was straight out of *West Side Story*. A tire iron suddenly appeared, then a set of tire chains, then a baseball bat, then another tire iron. Fairly equally armed for a fight to the death, the two groups faced off, hurling insults. Thankfully, and despite brain-numbing surges of testosterone, we still possessed enough of our wits to realize that if this went any further, someone *could* get killed, so it was quickly agreed that the best fighter from each crew would do battle, fists only. The lucky chosen ones circled each other, making the occasional feint, when suddenly police cars screamed down upon us from all four directions at once, obviously a carefully coordinated military maneuver designed to cut off any attempt at escape.

We were all arrested, taken to the local station, and booked. The desk sergeant began calling our parents. When he called mine, this is what we all heard:

"Hello, is this John Rosemond's mother? This is Sergeant O'Malley of the Westchester police. We have your son in custody for disturbing the peace and participating in a gang fight, and we'd like for you to come get him. . . . Yes, that's right. . . . He was arrested with eight other boys. . . . No, no one was hurt. . . . Yes, I can wait." And then, less than a minute later, "Yes, ma'am. . . . Well, that's somewhat unusual, but I suppose we can do that. How long would you like us to keep him?"

Everyone in the room turned in my direction, and someone said, "Rosemond, I think your parents are leaving you here."

Sure enough, they left me to rot in jail. My single-occupant cell was furnished with a sink, a toilet, and a metal cot. It lacked soap, towel, mattress, and blanket, and I was unable to persuade the jailer to provide them. After two nights that seemed like several months, my parents paid my bail and took me home, where I was confined for the remaining eight weeks of the summer, during which I washed walls, painted the exterior of our bungalow, and pulled every dandelion in our yard by hand. I never saw the other members of the Suburban Stupid Gang again.

During that summer, one of my stepfather's comments became stuck forever in my mind: "I knew if I gave you enough rope, you'd hang yourself." In other words, he and my mother disapproved of the company I was keeping, suspected our mischief would eventually come to the attention of John Law, and had probably even discussed the what-if of my arrest long before it actually happened. It sure didn't take them any time at all to make the decision to let me soak up the ambiance of a jail cell for a couple of days. In short, they were reasonably certain I was headed for big trouble but did absolutely nothing to prevent it. Their strategy was nothing short of brilliant.

Let's face it. Had my parents tried to prevent me, a high school graduate, from hanging with Terry and his crew, I would have found a way to hang with them anyway. Had they warned me that I was headed for all-but-certain legal trouble, I would have ignored them. They knew this, of course, and realized that teaching me the lesson I needed to learn required invoking the Long Rope Principle.

Needless to say, that entire experience made a huge imprint on me. Eighteen years later, my parents' brilliant strategy paid off for my son, Eric. At age fourteen, Eric took up with a group of boys that all lived in the most expensive gated neighborhood in our hometown and began spending every spare minute with them. One summer afternoon, I received a phone call from a friend who lived in the aforementioned enclave. He told me the boys Eric was running with were known vandals who had perpetrated considerable damage to various upscale homes, usually while the occupants were out of town. The boys' parents, enablers all, refused to accept that their kids were behind these crimes.

"I figured you'd want to know so you and Willie can put an end to the relationship before it goes any further," he said.

Willie and I talked and decided on a variation of my parents' long rope strategy. We sat down with Eric, told him what we had learned (without naming our informant, of course), and assured him we were going to do nothing to prevent him from continuing to associate with the boys in question.

"You can see them and be with them as much as you like," I said. I went on to explain that my anonymous friend had agreed to let me know the next time an act of vandalism occurred in his neighborhood.

"If such an act comes to our attention, Eric, and you cannot account for your whereabouts with a responsible adult witness, you will pay the victims the entire cost of their repairs. Even if the other boys' parents step up to the plate and pay their shares, you will still pay the entire amount, and you will be allowed to do nothing but earn money by doing work for other people until the entire amount is paid. In the meantime, you have our full permission to hang with those boys as much as you like."

Eric was looking at us like we'd just told him we were space aliens who had kidnapped his real parents and imprisoned them on a distant planet until he and his sister were old and wealthy enough to pay some impossibly huge ransom.

"Uh, okay" was all he said.

No more than two weeks later, I was mowing the grass when I looked up to see Eric racing down the street on his bike. When he reached our driveway, he sent his ride sliding into the grass as he hopped off and ran over to me.

"Dad! Dad!" he yelled. I turned off the mower. "Dad! I was with those guys, and they started planning something bad, and I told 'em I had to go to a dentist appointment and left, and Dad, believe me, if you hear something, I wasn't there, and Dad, I'm not going to hang with those guys ever again! I promise. I'm gonna find new friends!"

As I assured him I believed his story and told him how proud I was of him, I silently thanked my mom and stepdad for helping me, in the most paradoxical of ways, to be a better parent.

Again, had my parents made any attempt to keep me from hanging with the Suburban Stupid Gang, I would simply have taken the relationship underground. I'm sure the same would have been the case with Eric and the spoiled brats he'd taken up with. Who knows where those deceptions would have eventually led? In both cases, thankfully, application of the Long Rope Principle saved the day and prevented who knows what sort of trouble.

When I tell someone my age of my long rope story, it is more common than not for them to share a long rope story from their own childhood. We always agree that our parents' restraint was in our best interests, that it conveyed invaluable lessons that could not have been conveyed as effectively in any other way. In other words, those two days spent in jail were two of the most beneficial days of my life—and Eric's, too.

Today's parents, when they suspect their kids are headed

for trouble, swing into action. They do whatever is necessary to cut the trouble off at the proverbial pass. This knee-jerk reaction is certainly well intentioned, and there are certain situations in which it is appropriate. I am by no means suggesting that the Long Rope Principle be applied across the board. I am suggesting, however, that like letting children stew in their own juices and lie in beds they themselves make, giving children a long rope is sometimes the best of all parental strategies. It sure paid off handsomely for Eric. From then on, he chose his friends much, much more carefully.

The Bible Tells Me So!

The Bible tells of God employing the Long Rope Principle on numerous occasions, the first of which is in the Garden of Eden. He gives Adam and Eve, the first man and first woman, a single commandment and the freedom to break that commandment. Rather than hovering over their shoulders, he doesn't stick around to make sure they follow the rule—and allows them to make their own bad decision.

Many, many years later, Jesus employed the Long Rope Principle with Judas. Matthew's account of the Last Supper (26:17-30) makes perfectly clear that Jesus knew of Judas's betrayal. He knew all along, of course, and yet he allowed Judas to hold what was perhaps the highest administrative post within the disciples: treasurer. Furthermore, Jesus did nothing to dissuade Judas from his date with the devil, nothing to prevent him from doing what he did. Knowing full well what Judas was all about, he gave him a long rope. And sure enough, Judas hanged himself—literally.

God is not a micromanager. (I'm fully aware, by the way, that there are theologians who both agree and disagree with me on that issue, but I think most of them on both sides would agree that neither position is vital to salvation.) In that regard, God is a model of effective parenting. (Would we expect anything less?) Micromanaging parents are certainly motivated by the good intention of keeping their kids out of trouble. And there are indeed certain troubles that parents should do all they can to prevent. Nonetheless, when proper management crosses the line and becomes micromanagement, parents unwittingly deny their children immensely valuable learning experiences that come from feeling the consequences of their bad decisions.

To Ponder and Discuss

Can you identify a time or times when you intervened to head off trouble on behalf of one of your kids and in so doing prevented him or her from learning a lesson that only trouble can properly teach? Are there potentially problematic situations currently looming in your kids' lives that might call for the Long Rope Principle? What is one way you can both prevent the worst harm possible and still allow your children to learn what only bad consequences can teach?

6

"You Have to Learn to Stand on Your Own Two Feet"

My mother was a single parent for most of the first seven years of my life. During much of that time, we lived in a walk-up apartment in what is now the historic district of Charleston, South Carolina. (It would have been more accurately described as the run-down district back then.) She was a student at the College of Charleston and worked part time at the post office to make ends meet. She had a car—a 1950 English Anglia—but drove it sparingly. She mostly walked, so she understood, tangibly, the value of learning to stand on one's own two feet.

When she was a child, her parents had divorced. Her mother had taken her and her three younger siblings back to the family home—Rose Hill Plantation just outside of Hilton Head—where my mother remembered living for only a brief time until the state evicted them for failure (inability) to pay the tax on the property. Essentially homeless and without means of support, Grandmother Webb appealed to the Episcopal Church, who placed the children at the Episcopal Children's Home—an orphanage, essentially—in York, South Carolina. My mother spent most of her childhood and early teen years (during the Great Depression) there. She married when she was eighteen and right out of high school. My father was an outgoing, charming, talented man with deep-seated sociopathic tendencies that he didn't bring under control until he was in his sixties, when he found the Lord (better late than never!). My parents divorced when I was a toddler. Mom remarried when I was almost seven, and my stepfather, Julius, took us to Chicago. This was 1953. Talk about culture shock!

My mother's second marriage was a slow-motion disaster. Julius possessed an impressive intellect and a good sense of humor but was emotionally . . . well, the current term is "challenged." Like my mother, he'd experienced more than his share of hardship during the Depression. Empathy and compassion were not his strong suits. Nonetheless, my mother stayed with him, unwilling to admit to her family, I think, that she had made another bad matrimonial decision.

After living in apartments for several years, we moved into a modest bungalow in one of Chicago's suburbs, and Mom began attending college. She eventually earned her PhD in plant morphology, an esoteric branch of the life sciences, and she taught and did research until her retirement. She was a smart, pretty, and emotionally fragile woman. Life had beaten her up a lot. Mind you, her coping skills were considerable. They had simply been overwhelmed. This story ends well, however. After Julius passed, her dazzling personality gradually reemerged, and she began attending church. She passed peacefully at eighty-six, having found her way back to a relationship with Christ.

Determined to prepare me for life's slings and arrows, Mom was anything but an enabler. As a parent, she had a long-term vision, one she would remind me of on those occasions when I would come to her complaining of how difficult and unfair something was and asking her to solve whatever it was for me: "It's my job, John Rosemond, to help you learn to stand on your own two feet, and you are not going to learn to stand on yours if I let you stand on mine."

"But . . . but . . . but Mom!" I'd protest, searching for words that would change her mind.

"There'll be no buts about this," she would say. "Now run along."

One such occasion involved a fifth-grade math assignment. Stumped, I came to her complaining that I didn't understand the process and asking for her help. Mind you, I'm asking this of a woman who is a research scientist, mathematician, and statistician. For her, fifth-grade math was no big deal.

She took the book from me, turned several pages, and

then handed it back to me, saying, "I figured this out when I was your age, and so can you."

I was stunned. Then she said what has caused me to remember this encounter for life: "And let me remind you, when I was your age, I was in an orphanage. I had no one to go to for help, and I figured this out." And then she repeated, "So can you."

Being a child, I did not hear "so can you." I heard only that she was not going to give me any help. In other words, I heard her with the ears of a child. Obviously, the most important thing she said was "so can you." She was telling me that I did not need her help, that I was as smart and capable as she was, and that she was not about to cooperate in my "I can't" drama.

"Folly Is a Child"

Scripture says, "Foolishness is bound up in the heart of a child" (Proverbs 22:15). Children are drama factories, and many of their self-dramas are a variation of one sort or another on the "I can't" theme. Because they have short attention spans and their need for instant gratification is strong, when children encounter a difficult problem, they are not inclined to roll up their proverbial shirt sleeves and get to work. They fold. They complain. They produce drama, soap operas in which they are victims in desperate need of rescue. Most of this is foolishness, or as some translations of Proverbs 22:15 put it, folly.

Mom was not about to indulge my folly. She had a larger, more long-range vision of her purpose than was represented by the fifth-grade math assignment I was complaining about. If her vision had extended no further into the future than the grade I was going to receive the next day on my assignment, she would have helped me. But her purpose was not about a fifth-grade math assignment; it was about the assignments and problems I would encounter as an adult.

But the story's not over. Upon hearing her remind me that she had been in an orphanage, and hearing her with the ears of a child, and wanting her to enable rather than challenge the foolishness in my heart, I said, "But Mom! I know you were in an orphanage, but this isn't an orphanage! This is our house, and you're not some orphanage lady. You're my mother, and you know how to do this stuff, and I'm just asking for your help!"

And she calmly said, "Well, I've already told you, I'm not going to help you, and that's that." And then, with a wave of her hand, she said, "Now run along." And I was dismissed from Her Majesty's presence. I am reasonably certain that after much gnashing of teeth and blaspheming of my mother under my breath, I figured out the assignment. Generally speaking, children are much, much more capable than they think they are.

After a talk during which I had told this story, a woman approached me and asked, "What if you really had not been able to figure it out, John? Would your mother have helped you then?"

This was a good question, and my answer was and is "I honestly doubt it." This was, after all, a woman who once made me sit at the dinner table until I finally, close to midnight, worked up the courage to eat a few forkfuls of broccoli. She was much more determined than I was. Her strength of will could better mine on my most obstinate days. Had I not been able to figure out the problem, and had I come to her in tears an hour or so later, I'm fairly certain she would have said something along these lines: "No one solves all the problems life throws at them. If you don't figure out that math assignment, your life won't end."

In other words, Mom was not concerned with whether I succeeded on a fifth-grade assignment; she was concerned with whether I succeeded at life. In that regard, I needed to learn that a) I was not going to solve all the problems life threw at me, b) I must choose whether failure to solve some problem is a positive or negative experience, c) I must determine, always, to do my best, and d) failure becomes a failing only if I choose.

People succeed at life not because of strong math skills; they succeed at life because of strength of character. That was Mom's purpose. As a parent, she was farsighted. It paid off for both of us. I emancipated and married my wife-for-life, Willie, when I was twenty. I was a parent, supporting a family of three, at twenty-one. I have lots of shortcomings, Lord knows, but not being able to stand on my own two feet is not one of them.

Thanks, Ma.

The Bible Tells Me So!

The people complained in the hearing of the LORD
about their misfortunes, and when the LORD
heard it, his anger was kindled, and the fire of
the LORD burned among them and consumed
some outlying parts of the camp. Then the people
cried out to Moses, and Moses prayed to the LORD, and the fire
died down.
—*NUMBERS 11:1-2, ESV*

Do all things without complaining and disputing.
—*PHILIPPIANS 2:14*

Standing on one's own two feet requires perseverance. Perseverance requires us to push through, rather than grumble, even (and especially) when circumstances are difficult. The Bible is full of stories of people who persevered and eventually succeeded in the face of tremendous adversity. To cite one prominent example, can you just imagine what the world would be like today if twenty or so years into the seemingly endless wandering the Lord had meted out to the Israelites, Moses had said, "I've had enough of these people! My feet are worn out, and so is my patience, and I'm tired of eating nothing but this manna stuff! I'm done!" What would have happened if he had taken his rod and robe and gone back to a reasonably comfortable life herding livestock in Midian? The prophets—all of them—are exemplars of perseverance.

None of them gave up, even though that would have been the "logical" choice.

But there are no better examples of a tenacious spirit than the disciples. When the mob stoned Stephen, the disciples would have had every right to return to their previously comfortable lives as fishermen and so on. Instead, they never complained. They pushed on, knowing that horrible earthly fates lay just down the road. God wants believers who will stand up and stand strong in the face of whatever hardships the world throws their way. The earlier that training begins, the better.

To Ponder and Discuss

Do you think you're doing a good job of helping your children learn to stand on their own two feet? If not, what can you do to help your children develop that spirit? Perhaps more important, what can you *stop* doing? Are there problems or issues in your children's lives where you've been too helpful, perhaps to the point of becoming an enabler? What excuses on your part are rationalizing and supporting that enabling? How might allowing your children to figure things out on their own improve these problems and issues?

7

"You Will Have to Learn Your Lessons the Hard Way"

According to my parents, I was going to have to learn my lessons the hard way because I had a thick skull and potatoes in my ears. Sometimes, however, my auditory canals must have been clear of potatoes, because the things they told me went in one ear and out the other. My parents did not seem the least bit concerned about my cranial and auditory infirmities, however. They knew their influence in my life did not extend to such things. Therefore, I was going to have to learn certain lessons the hard way. They were, as usual, precisely on the money.

Today's parents, by contrast, seem to believe that if they use proper words in a proper sequence, they can cause their children to understand the life lessons they are trying to communicate.

"What can I say to my son," asked the mother of a fourteen-year-old, "to help him understand that by trying harder in school, he increases his chances of getting into a good college?"

"How can I get my daughter," asked the father of a ten-year-old, "to understand that she is causing her own social difficulties by bossing other girls around?"

"Are there words I can use," asked the mother of a seventeen-year-old, "to help my daughter understand that she doesn't need attention from boys to feel worthwhile?"

Parents frequently ask me these sorts of questions. In each of these real-life examples, the parent can see the problem clearly and desperately wants to help the child understand and solve it. In each case, the parent is motivated by nothing but love for the child. And in each case, the parent is searching for words that don't exist, because in each case, the child has a hard head and potatoes clogging his or her ears and is, therefore, going to have to learn the needed lesson the hard way, through firsthand experience with certain facts of life.

Knowing this simple and timeless truth, parents of old dedicated themselves not to making happiness in their children's lives but to making reality. They gave children freedom to fall flat on their faces (or, as my parents sometimes put it, "enough rope to hang yourself"), knowing that children must fall down before they learn how not to fall down and must mess up in order to grow up.

Many of today's parents, by contrast, believe that failure

in any form chips away large chunks of a child's self-esteem. As a consequence, they protect their kids from reality to such an extent that those kids don't learn what reality is until they're young adults. Then, in order to avoid dealing with it for the longest possible time, they continue to live at home until . . . who knows when?

Since 1976, the percentage of children twenty-two and older still living at home, largely dependent upon parental support, has doubled. It's clear that many of these children are looking for an indefinite extension of the guarantee their parents have always provided. To wit: you will never have to learn anything the hard way.

In the above examples, there is no amount of parental talk that will cause the child in question to understand what the parent wants him or her to understand. No words will suddenly penetrate the child's thick skull or drill through the child's ear potatoes and cause said child to suddenly exclaim, "Mom! Dad! I get it! You're absolutely right! Wow! Thank you for helping me understand I've been on the wrong path. This conversation has been life changing! I love you guys!"

Nope. Children will understand the life lessons their parents want them to understand when they are adults—make that when they are the parents of children their present age. Someday the child with ear potatoes will be a parent trying to get a child with ear potatoes to understand something that a child cannot understand. Which is why "You're going to have to learn certain things the hard way" is as valid today as it was in the 1950s, when I first heard it.

And by the way, I did not have a clue what my parents were talking about. *The hard way? What's that?* I finally figured out what it meant, courtesy of more than one "hard way" experience. During the early years of our marriage, Willie and I endured my being fired from two jobs (I had a huge problem with authority), living hand-to-mouth with two children (but we always managed to pay our bills), and suffering the almost-inevitable emotional consequences of marrying young and having two children before we'd completely adjusted to just being married. We now realize that through these physical and emotional hardships, the Lord was preparing us for a ministry assignment. He "hardened" us, if you will, with one hard way after another.

This probably sounds strange, but bear with me, please: I love going through the checkout line at grocery stores. I don't even mind having to wait on someone ahead of me who has a cart overflowing with what looks like enough food to feed an army for a month, because I get a kick out of reading the covers of the various tabloids in the checkout racks. I am always amused by the latest dramas coming out of Hollywood—stupid affairs (pardon the redundancy), marriages on the rocks, messy divorces, child custody and alimony battles, botched plastic surgeries, weight issues ("Traumatized by Winning an Oscar, So-and-So Loses Eighty Pounds, Then Gains Two Hundred!"), wrinkle issues ("Once-Glamorous Star Now Afraid to Be Seen in Public!"), bankruptcies, crazy relatives ("My Mother Stole All My Money!"), phobias, childhood traumas ("I Can Finally Admit It: I Failed

Kindergarten!"), mansions slowly sliding off seaside cliffs, nervous breakdowns, not-so-nervous breakdowns—the list goes on and on, creating the impression that no one on the planet lives or has ever lived a tougher life than a grossly over-paid Hollywood celebrity. Yes, cynical as it may be, standing in the checkout line is one of my favorite recreations.

The celebrities who populate these tabloid covers are in serious need of some real hardship, like the hardship of being a West Virginia coal miner with a wife and five kids whose mine just closed because a bunch of pampered politicians decided that burning coal is politically incorrect. Or the hardship of being a Christian in Africa who lives with the constant fear of persecution by people representing a certain religion that I cannot mention because its adherents might be offended. Or the hardship of being the wife of an American soldier who has been killed in battle in some desert country halfway around the globe. Or for that matter, the hardship of being an American soldier who is fighting in some desert country halfway around the globe to advance the cause of freedom for people he doesn't know and who may not appreciate his sacrifice. The point is, there is real hardship in this broken world, but its address is not in Hollywood.

Valuable lessons are learned the hard way. In fact, the harder the way, the more valuable the lesson. One of the responsibilities of being a parent is to protect children from hardships they truly cannot handle. It's equally true, however, that one of the responsibilities of being a parent is to prepare children for hardship. That is done by simply letting them have a controlled taste, every now and then, of what real life is all about by letting them fall flat on their faces, run into proverbial brick walls, be disappointed, experience failure, be rejected, not be chosen, be treated unfairly, and so on. Doing bad things to children is pure evil, but preparing children for bad stuff is an act of love.

The Bible Tells Me So!

Count it all joy, my brothers, when you meet trials of various kinds, for you know that the testing of your faith produces steadfastness. And let steadfastness have its full effect, that you may be perfect and complete, lacking in nothing.
—JAMES 1:2-4, ESV

Indeed, all who desire to live a godly life in Christ Jesus will be persecuted.
—2 TIMOTHY 3:12, ESV

A currently popular saying has it that "life is hard and then you die." It's a bit of an exaggeration—for most people, that is—but it effectively makes the point that life is not a bed of roses or a bowl of cherries. At the very least, life's a bed of roses that conceals many thorns or a bowl of cherries with some deadly nightshade thrown in for good measure.

The Bible makes it as clear as clear can be that nothing good in this life is ever achieved except through hard work and hardship. Life's hardships, if endured properly with a heart turned toward Christ, usually have positive outcomes beyond expectation, including the most positive and glorious outcome of all: eternal life with God.

To Ponder and Discuss

Have you done too good a job of protecting your children from hardship? Have you broken too many falls, too often prevented them from coming into contact with brick walls, righted all the wrongs in their lives, and made sure everything that happened to them was fair? Do you think you can prepare them for real life simply by talking to them? Does it seem, more often than not, that your talking is falling on deaf ears? Are you ready to stop talking so much and begin helping them develop the coping skills they are going to need to deal with life's inevitable misfortunes? What can you do within the next week to begin that process?

8

"Every Child Has a Mind of His Own"

Sigmund Freud, the so-called "Father of Modern Psychology," popularized the idea that the manner in which a child is raised determines the adult he or she becomes, that parenting produces the person. Freud used hypnosis, primarily, to help his patients reconnect with childhood experiences that he believed (and persuaded his patients to believe) had shaped their personalities and were responsible for whatever symptoms they presented. Although none of Freud's theories have been proved, they are still taught in university psychology programs as if they contain significant validity, when they are really nothing more than the wild speculations of a person who was himself, by all accounts, fairly troubled.

Freud's theories are why psychologists probe the child-hoods of their patients. They're attempting to make cause-and-effect connections between the various emotional problems that adults bring to their attention and the manner in which those adults were raised. And of course, no matter what sort of childhood a particular patient had—good, bad, or unremarkable—a psychologist will discover a connection.

Freud's deterministic theories made the jump from academia to popular culture in the 1950s and 1960s. As a consequence, parents slowly became convinced that parenting errors on their part had the potential to mess their kids up for life. Furthermore, no parent could escape the wide throw of Freud's net. The strict parent who enforced high standards was raising a future obsessive-compulsive neurotic, while the permissive, relaxed parent was raising an adult who would bounce from identity crisis to identity crisis, never able to figure out a clear purpose to his or her life. In between were parents who raised run-of-the-mill, garden-variety, plain-old messed-up people.

Prior to the popularization of Freudian theory, parents understood that children will sometimes (and for some children, often) do things that are completely unrelated to anything their parents have or have not done. In other words, children will misbehave and do various odd, inexplicable things no matter what. Parents can minimize the possibility, perhaps, but not eliminate it.

A dog trainer once told me that "you train children the same way you train dogs." I told him there are fundamental differences. For example, if someone trains a puppy properly, it will never be a problem. With children, however, all bets are off. Parents can train children properly, and the children will still occasionally be a problem, and maybe even more often than just occasionally. The difference between puppies and children is the latter's free will—minds of their own.

Today's parents—mothers, especially—tend to believe that parenting produces the child (and by extension, the person the child becomes). They believe, in other words, that children do *not* have minds of their own, that they are the sum total of their parents' actions toward them. The only thing this Freudian falsehood produces is tremendous anxiety and guilt for mothers.

Why mothers and not so much fathers? Because, generally speaking, men do not consume parenting materials. Overwhelmingly, women are the primary consumers of parenting stuff, most of which qualifies as unmitigated babble. As a consequence, it is primarily women whose thinking becomes infected with the misinformation, unfounded theories, and downright dumb advice that characterizes most of the babble in question. As they read parenting materials (not all, mind you, but definitely most), women open their brains to invasion by what I call "psychological bogeymen," which most of today's parenting books and magazines are full of. These bogeymen scrabble around in their brains, drowning out the calming voice of good, old-fashioned, nonintellectual common sense.

Women of my mother's generation and earlier did not believe they had to read in order to be good mothers. They believed child rearing was a natural process God had equipped human beings to do (the way he had also equipped geese and wolves and dogs and cats and elephants to do), and any responsible person could be trusted to do it reasonably well. Those women were also familiar with the Genesis story of Adam and Eve, in which we learn that the one and only perfect Parent there is or ever will be creates two children who disobey his first instruction. As soon as their Father's back is turned, those two first children do the very worst thing they could have possibly done. What parenting fault in God caused this fault in his first kids? None, because God has no faults. Therefore, the only possible explanation for Adam and Eve's misbehavior is that "every child has a mind of his own."

No matter how well, by any standard, children are raised, they are still capable of engaging in all manner of egregious behavior. In Psalm 51:5, David writes, "Surely I was sinful at birth, sinful from the time my mother conceived me" (NIV). Human beings are inclined toward sin, toward doing what is self-gratifying without regard for others, from day one. Human beings are moral relativists by nature. Mothers of three-plus generations ago, when biblical principles still held sway in America, understood that no amount of good mothering could neutralize that inconvenient fact. Children, it was generally agreed, were fundamentally bad. They could not be made good; they could only be taught, through firm discipline lovingly applied, to control their badness and do more good things than bad things. At best, we are bad people who have learned, contrary to our natures, to act properly.

And then Freud came along, and in the process of attempting to understand his own very odd self, he proposed that bad behavior was the result of bad parenting. He came up with a cockamamy theory to the effect that children's psychological development occurred in three stages: oral, anal, and phallic (don't even ask how such nonsense applies to girls). Almost invariably, parents (more specifically, *mothers*) responded inappropriately to one or more of these stages—the mother didn't breast-feed long enough, her toilet training methods were punitive, or she caused her boys to feel shame for having penises—and as a result, children became walking basket cases of one sort or another. In Freud's view, the concept of Original Sin was a primitive attempt at understanding what he alone was smart enough to finally get right. (And yes, by all accounts he was a raging megalomaniac who believed his thoughts were truth.) Human beings did not need Christ (or any religious mythology for that matter); rather, they needed therapy. Thus, psychology became a secular religion, and psychologists became personal saviors. And mothers became beset by anxiety and plagued by guilt. And men stood by, wondering what in the world was going on.

Freud's cockamamy theories have produced lots of anxiety and nagging guilt for women, and they have also resulted in mothers being extremely defensive concerning their children.

Teachers frequently ask me why today's moms have such difficulty accepting that their kids sometimes misbehave. My answer: "Because whether they know it or not, they believe Freud." They believe that badness in their kids reflects badly on them. Unlike my mother and other women B.F. (Before Freud), they are threatened by reports that their kids have behaved badly. They take these reports personally.

When my mom received a report from school that I had misbehaved in class or on the playground, her response was "Thanks for the report. I will take care of it. Anytime John steps out of line, let me know." She was not surprised or threatened. She did not think bad behavior from John meant she had fallen down on the job; therefore, she did not respond defensively.

Today's all-too-typical mom, upon hearing a report of school misbehavior, becomes her child's advocate and attorney. Her child, she maintains, was unjustly accused, and even if she admits that her child did whatever the teacher is reporting, she insists it is someone else's fault—even the teacher's! The mother's defensiveness is her way of keeping at bay the nagging feeling that if the teacher's report is accurate, then she is to blame. My mother heard a report about me; today's mom hears a report about herself.

I am most definitely not saying that parents are never to blame when it comes to their children's misbehavior. Some parents send completely undisciplined children to school. Most of those parents, when teachers or principals report misbehavior, also become defensive. So we have parents who become defensive for the wrong reason and parents who become defensive for the right reason. What a mess!

All of this means that lots of children, a lot of the time, are not being held accountable for their misdeeds. That guarantees that school behavior problems are going to increase—and indeed they have, dramatically so since the days when children had minds of their own.

Someone once remarked to me that school behavior was not a problem when teachers were allowed to paddle their students. I disagreed. Paddling had nothing to do with good school behavior. I went to schools where paddles were not used, and yet kids were no less well behaved than they were at schools I attended where paddling was allowed. It wasn't paddles that made the difference; it was parental support. When children were punished at school, they were punished at home. There was never a question of whether the teacher had reported the problem accurately and never a question of whether the child, therefore, deserved to be punished. We should all hope for a return of those days.

"But what if a teacher is wrong about something, John?" you might ask. "What if she *has* blamed the wrong child?"

"Well, that presents the child's parents with a golden opportunity to teach the child that life's not fair," I would respond. (For more on that, see the next chapter.)

Parents are an influence in a child's life and development. They are not the sole influence, and sometimes, through no fault of their own, they are not the biggest influence. For sure, they are the biggest influence when the child is young, but as a child grows, more and more influences—peers, teachers, coaches, random (unpredictable) experiences, his or her physical development, to name but a few—leave their mark. But no influence is ever as powerful as the child's own free will.

A parent once asked, "When does the child's free will begin asserting itself?"

"The reputation two-year-olds have for being defiant," I answered, "is a symptom of a free will that is already, a mere two years into the child's upbringing, a powerful force to be reckoned with." Toddlers most definitely have minds of their own. They hit other children in their preschool program even though their parents have carefully insulated them from violence of any sort. As soon as they develop speech, they begin to lie, even though their parents have never lied to them (and, interestingly enough, a child's first lie is a variation on the first lie ever told: "I didn't do it!"). Their parents have been nothing but generous with them, yet they will not share with anyone else. Their parents have a demonstrably loving relationship, yet they demonstrate nothing but resentment toward their siblings. The list goes on. Much to their parents' chagrin, at times, children have minds of their own. They are going to do things their way, in their time, at their pace, if they consent to do them at all.

The fact that children have minds of their own means they are responsible for their own behavior. If their minds were nothing more than biological computers that their parents and other adults programmed, then personal responsibility would be a fiction.

Make no mistake: parents make mistakes, and some parents make big mistakes that do leave fairly indelible marks on their kids. But when all is said and done, Grandma was right once again!

The Bible Tells Me So!

Who did not have a mind of his or her own in the Bible? Why, no one! Adam and Eve surely had minds of their own, as did Cain. The history of mankind is largely the history of the self-destructive means and ends to which God's children have put their own minds. God speaks directly to and inspires certain people—the prophets, for instance—but he does not ever take over someone's brain and turn that person into a mere automaton. Likewise, parents are an influence; they are not the whole story.

To Ponder and Discuss

As a child, did you ever misbehave in ways that had absolutely nothing to do with anything your parents had or had not done, that bore no relation whatsoever to the values they were trying to train into you? If your misbehavior was not a matter of bad parenting, what was it? Have your children ever done weird, strange, odd, bad, and perhaps even downright evil things that cannot possibly be explained in terms of mistakes you have made as a parent? What explains these things?

9

"Life's Not Fair"

In Grandma's day, when children complained that some circumstance in life wasn't fair—their teacher gave them a grade they thought they didn't deserve, another kid won the spelling bee because he was given easier words, they had to do their chores before they could join their friends outside—the parents to whom they directed this complaint would simply say, "Life's not fair."

When one of my parents said that to me, I would grind my teeth together. It was infuriating. In my childish mind, fair was nothing less than right. Furthermore, since it was *my* life at issue, I alone held the privilege of defining what was fair and not fair. Therefore, if I thought something was not fair, that was that; it was wrong and needed to be corrected! And since I obviously couldn't correct it on my own, my parents should correct it for me. But instead of seeing things from my perspective—which was the *right* perspective, of course—they just shook their heads and told me that life isn't fair. *That* wasn't fair either. Fair was that they would see my point of view and make things right in my life again.

It took adulthood and then parenthood for me to learn that to a child, fair is winning, being first, getting the biggest slice of cake, making the highest score on the test, and that sort of thing. From a child's point of view, fair has nothing to do with equitable or right. It means the child gets what the child wants, when he or she wants it. The childish belief that life should be "fair" is, therefore, nothing more than an expression of the child's inherent self-centeredness. From a theological perspective, a child's complaints of unfairness are nothing more than expressions of his sinful nature.

From yet another perspective, however, "life's not fair" is a simple statement of fact. After all, there's nothing fair about life. Big Government politicians and bureaucrats have tried and will continue to try to make fairness mandatory, but they have failed and will continue to fail. From the bottom up, unfairness is the natural state of things. If life were fair, monkeys would eat as many tigers as tigers eat monkeys. The list of unfairness is endless. Sharks and parrot fish, falcons and hummingbirds, swallows and insects, humans and cows, bigger humans and smaller humans, faster humans and slower humans, highly intelligent humans and humans with average

IQs, hardworking humans and lazy humans—someone or something is always getting the short end of the stick. Ironically, the earlier in life we accept and come to grips with this three-word fact, the happier we will be. I say it's ironic, because let's face it: unfairness is not something to celebrate. It's the inescapable result of two unalterable facts: 1) this world is broken, and 2) humans are fallen creatures. It's not *a* reality, as in *one aspect of*; it's *the* reality of material life.

"Life's not fair" is also parents' means of informing children that they are not going to solve whatever it is that has gotten the better of the children. Parents would, in fact, be doing children a disservice if they did solve the problem for them. As truly happy people know, happiness depends not only on their acceptance of life's unfairness but also on their acceptance of personal responsibility—understanding that in the final analysis, no one is going to solve life's problems for them; they are going to have to figure them out on their own.

Grandma did not believe it was her responsibility to solve all of her children's problems, relieve all of their distress, or intervene in their lives such that they only experienced that which they thought was fair. Many of today's parents, by contrast, believe that those responsibilities are part of their job description and that living out these responsibilities defines the good parent. Grandma told her kids that life wasn't fair and nothing she could do was going to make it so. Today's parents tell their kids, in effect, that life *should* treat them fairly and that when it doesn't, then by gosh and by golly, they are going to set things right. When Grandma said,

"Life's not fair," she said it with compassion, knowing that her children were going to experience suffering, disappointment, and even failure. By no means did she relish that outcome. She simply knew that her children needed a healthy dose of reality at that moment.

Mind you, Grandma was not going to let her children suffer indiscriminately. She was going to prevent them, as toddlers, from running into the street. She was going to do all she could to prevent her children from experiencing devastating emotional or physical injury. She was going to make sure they did not, as children, experience levels of suffering, disappointment, and failure that only adults can be expected to endure. There's a huge difference between a parent who relishes seeing children suffer and a parent who allows children to experience a reasonable amount of suffering in order to advance their maturity. The former is a sadist; the latter is a compassionate and responsible life coach.

Vitamin N

"That's not fair!" is one of childhood's battle cries—things children say and questions they ask for the sole purpose of luring unsuspecting, well-intentioned adults into no-win verbal exchanges that always, without exception, result in these adults—slow learners all—undermining their own authority. "Why?" and "Why not?" have held and forever will continue to hold the top two slots for childhood battle cries (see chapter 1). "That's not fair!" comes in a close third.

Children employ the "That's not fair!" strategy primarily in response to a) not getting what they want, b) being told to do what they do not want to do, and c) being punished unjustly (or so the child thinks). First, an example of the unfairness of not getting what the child wants:

> **Tommy (age eight):** Mom? Dad? Can I have chocolate ice cream for dinner?
>
> **Tommy's father (age forty-eight):** No, you cannot.
>
> **Tommy:** But Billy's parents let him eat ice cream for dinner sometimes! He told me so!
>
> **Tommy's father:** Then it must be true. Don't you think, honey? If Billy said it, it must be true?
>
> **Tommy's mother (age undeterminable):** Absolutely. No question about it.
>
> **Tommy:** So can I, then?
>
> **Tommy's father:** No.
>
> **Tommy:** That's not fair!

If you have children, that exchange probably sounds familiar. Like all children, when Tommy says a decision his parents have made isn't fair, what he really means is that he is entitled to whatever he wants. If he wants ice cream for dinner, then he should receive ice cream for dinner, and anything less is a miscarriage of justice.

I have often—in print and in public presentations— compared young children to sociopaths. If that's shocking to the reader, I understand, and I ask only that you bear with me. Sociopaths, you see, think like young children, and vice versa. Both sociopaths and young children believe:

1. What they want, they deserve to have.
2. Because they deserve whatever "it" is, the ends justify the means.
3. Because they deserve whatever "it" is, no one has a right to deny them or stand in their way.
4. Because they are "special cases," the rules other people should obey do not apply to them.

Those four points describe, to the proverbial T, the way toddlers think. If you've lived with a toddler, then you recognize the description. As children mature in their thinking, courtesy of proper discipline from parents, teachers, and other caring adults, they begin to think "outside themselves." They begin to take other people into consideration before they act. They begin to realize, however intuitively, that the world is a safe and secure place if and only if people agree to obey the rules and accept no for an answer. Slowly, sociopathic thinking is replaced by socialized thinking. But it takes eighteen years or so to adequately socialize children, to scrub most of the sociopath out of their character. Fortunately, most of the sociopath is scrubbed out of most children by age eighteen. Unfortunately, the sociopath is never scrubbed out of some people. These unfortunates are toddlers for life. To them, life isn't fair unless they are getting whatever they want, and if getting it requires breaking laws as well as taking advantage of and even hurting other people, well, it is what it is. They deserve it, and that's that.

I've just explained why God does not allow human beings to grow to full size within two years. He designed that feature into most other species but not humans. Why? Because young children are sociopaths, and sociopaths are dangerous. Saying no to a two-year-old human who is two feet tall and weighs twenty-four pounds is one thing. Saying no to a two-year-old human who is six feet tall and weighs one hundred fifty pounds would be quite another thing. Can you imagine what that two-year-old's tantrums would look like or what the consequences of those tantrums would be to his parents? God is merciful, amen.

Another parenting pundit once told an audience that I believed in "might makes right"—that if it took physical force to control a child, John Rosemond was all for it. My initial reaction to that was defensive, but the more I thought about it, the more I had to agree. Sometimes all a toddler understands is physical force. I'm by no means referring to hurting the child, but I am definitely saying that there are times when toddlers require physical restraint. If that's what it takes to bring a toddler under control, there is absolutely nothing wrong with a loving parent providing it.

One day when my oldest grandchild was two, he began to throw a wild, thrashing tantrum at my house because Willie and I would not obey his commands. He zipped quickly past the point where he could restore control to himself, so I restored it for him. I gently (but with physical force) put him on the floor, immobilized him, and said, in a gentle voice, "I'm going to hold you here, Jack, until you stop screaming." He stopped screaming almost immediately. Two weeks later, he was at our house again and began to throw a tantrum because we would not cooperate in his entitlement fantasy. I held him by his upper arm and said, "Do you want to go to the floor again?" His eyes got big and wide and he stopped, mid-scream. And that was that. Yep. Sociopaths understand force.

Toddlers throw physical and verbal tantrums when they don't get their way. In most cases, properly disciplined eight-year-olds like Tommy usually throw only very brief verbal tantrums. They usually sound like "That's not fair!" which simply means that there's still a sociopath lurking down deep inside, a sociopath who believes that what the child wants, the child deserves to have.

The lingering sociopath's fingers must be slowly pried loose from their grip on children's character. The word *no* is the most essential aspect of this prying. It should be said a lot because the more it is said—and meant—the more quickly the prying proceeds. For every time parents say yes to children, they should say no at least five times. Eight is even better. Keep in mind, however, that no is not just a word. It is a concept that twentieth-century philosopher and bon vivant Mick Jagger expressed thus: "You can't always get what you want, but if you try sometimes, you just might find you get what you need." The concept is meaningless, vapid, empty, insipid, and other terms along those lines unless—and only unless—parents stand behind the word, and stand firm.

Children have an inalienable right to discover whether their parents mean what they say. They make this discovery by reacting in various antisocial ways when their parents say no. They yell, scream, cry, sob, stomp, jump up and down, twirl around dramatically, fall in a heap on the floor even more dramatically, attempt to start an argument, make disrespectful remarks, say they "hate" their parents, and so on. When parents say no, if they also react to these various and sundry discovery strategies by standing firm, then children become convinced, sooner or later, that their parents mean what they say, and these discovery strategies—also known as "testing"—slowly stop. If, on the other hand, children discover they can wear their parents down and cause them to give in, then these discovery strategies get worse, and worse, and worse, and where the worsening will eventually stop is anyone's bet. We all know adults who still have not learned that no means no.

Rebellion in Disguise

The second occasion when children employ the "It's not fair!" ploy is when their parents or teachers tell them to do something that not every other child in the entire scope of history has been required to do. In this case, what children really mean is "I don't want to!" Don't be fooled—this use of "It's not fair" is actually a clever form of disobedience. At the very least, it's an attempt to disobey. The following exchange between six-year-old Lucretia and her mother is typical:

Lucretia's mother: Lucretia, I need you to set the table for dinner, please.

Lucretia: Why do I always have to do everything?

Lucretia's mother: Because you were born to serve me and obey my every command.

Lucretia: No! I wasn't! And I shouldn't have to! Martine's mother doesn't make her set the table and stuff!

Lucretia's mother: But I'm not asking you to set the table and stuff. I'm asking you only to set the table. You're getting off easy this time.

Lucretia: It's not fair!

Lucretia's mother: Honey, I've told you before that the fair happens only once a year, and today isn't the day.

Lucretia: I don't know what that means!

Lucretia's mother: It means you have to set the table. Now.

Lucretia: It's not fair!

I'll bet that exchange rings a few bells for you. The most important thing about this not-so-hypothetical parenting drama is that Lucretia's mother stands her ground. She tells Lucretia to set the table and does not waver in the face of Lucretia's demand to be accorded the same privilege as her friend. The second most important thing is that Lucretia's mother has a sense of humor. I'm sure you couldn't help but notice that Tommy's parents also have a sense of humor. Nothing, and I mean not one other single thing, will help you endure the slings and arrows of raising children as much as a sense of humor, an appreciation of the absurd. Children, let's face it, are often absurd. The fact that they take themselves so very seriously is the most outstanding feature of their absurdity.

Because she has such a great sense of humor, Lucretia's mother has come up with a wonderfully creative alternative to "Life's not fair." This is one instance when altering the original wording of a traditional parenting aphorism can be justified.

"The fair happens only once a year, and today isn't the day" has panache. A woman once told me that's what her parents said every time she complained that a decision they made wasn't fair. One day, when she was about five years old, her mother came into her room in the morning and told her to get up and get dressed because "today's the day!"

"The day for what?" the little girl asked.

"The day fair happens!" her mother exclaimed. "I'm so excited! Hurry up! Time's a-wastin'!"

You can no doubt anticipate the rest of the story. The girl's parents took her to the county fair that day. On the way home, they reminded her that fair wouldn't happen again for another year. She told me she never said, "That's not fair!" ever again. Now, those were two parents after my own heart!

The More Things Change . . .

The third and final use of "It's not fair" is when children are punished for something they did but insist they did not do or insist that there were circumstances that gave them no choice in the matter. Consider this example:

God: Did you do what I specifically told you not to do? Did you eat from that tree over there, the one I specifically told you not to eat from?

Adam, then Eve: Well, sort of. I mean, uh, yeah, kind of, but not really, because I didn't mean to, and besides, I was under the spell of a bad influence, so it doesn't count . . . does it?

God: There'll be no ifs, ands, or buts about this. You did what I told you not to do, and I only tell you once, and now it's time for me to lower the boom. This is going to hurt me more than it hurts you, but you can't stay here any longer. I'm kicking you out.

Adam and Eve (in chorus): That's not fair!

God: Oy vey! I can see where this is going.

Thousands of years later, children are still the same. They still have great difficulty accepting that they can't get whatever they want and do whatever they feel like doing. They still can't accept that the world's not a bowl of prepitted cherries constantly replenished by a cosmic butler, that they can't always walk on the sunny side of the street, and that fair only comes once a year.

But when all is said and done, that's what makes 'em so lovable.

The Bible Tells Me So!

Fret not yourself because of evildoers; be not envious of wrongdoers! For they will soon fade like the grass and wither like the green herb. Trust in the LORD, and do good; dwell in the land and befriend faithfulness. Delight yourself in the LORD, and he will give you the desires of your heart. Commit your way to the LORD; trust in him, and he will act.
—PSALM 37:1-5, ESV

One of the recurrent themes in the Bible is that bad things happen to good people. Consider Job, to whom all manner of bad things happened that all would agree he did not deserve. We also learn from Scripture that God visits "unfairness" on good people as a means of testing them, strengthening their faith, and causing them to turn away from faith in their own sufficiency and turn instead to him. Despair, therefore, in the face of life's unfairness is an act of unfaithfulness. It is the consequence of believing that worldly problems have worldly solutions and feeling that all is lost when no worldly solution seems to work.

To Ponder and Discuss

Do your children frequently complain that things in their lives are not fair? Have you attempted to make life fair for them? Do you try to right all the perceived wrongs in their lives? Do you try to ensure that, as much as possible, things will turn out in their favor? Do you get "sucked in" to their unhappiness over life's inherent unfairness? Can you now see this as an indication that there is not a sufficient emotional boundary between you and your children? What can you now do to put that boundary in place and help your children accept that life simply isn't fair and that no amount of effort on your part can make it so?

10

"You're Acting Too Big for Your Britches"

"You'd better size yourself to those britches right now, John Rosemond, or I'm gonna size 'em to you!"

That's the way I heard it from my mother from fairly early on. On every such occasion, I was attracting undue attention to myself—and "undue" meant any attention at all. Those were the days when children were not supposed to act like the situation they were in was all about them— especially if adults were involved. This was before instilling high self-esteem into children became parents' raison d'être, before parents began thinking it was cute to have three-year-olds entertain adults with renditions of popular country songs.

Related aphorisms included "You must think the world

revolves around you" and "You'd better get down off that high horse before I snatch you down!" Each had a slightly different nuance, so they were used in slightly different contexts.

"You're acting too big for your britches" meant the children in question were either attracting undue attention to themselves or were puffed up with pride over some accomplishment—a good grade on a test, for example. In either case, they no longer fit into their britches—figuratively, of course. Even girls were told this, long before girls even wore britches.

"You must think the world revolves around you" was a rebuke typically used when children obviously thought their preference or taste should hold sway in a situation. The children were displeased with the restaurant their parents had chosen, for example, and made their dissatisfaction disrespectfully known.

Telling children they needed to get down off their high horse had a similar meaning to telling them they were acting too big for their britches. In this case, however, the children had affected a superior attitude, had gotten a "big head" (used in the same context) over some accomplishment, such as winning a game.

Underlying all of these reprimands was the understanding that humility and modesty are virtues. This was the day when children were also told, "It's not whether you win or lose; it's how you play the game." Character was more important than accomplishment. Win or lose, they were to do so graciously and not crow about their successes. They weren't to "toot their own horns." If they won a game, they were to congratulate their opponent for excellent play.

It was relatively easy for me to make As in school (which I later realized was not necessarily an advantage). If my parents told me once, they told me a thousand times not to brag about my grades. It was rude, they said. It made other people feel bad; therefore, it was disrespectful. If others asked what grade I'd made on a test, I was to simply tell them I'd done okay.

In the early 1970s, psychologists and other mental health "experts" began beating the drum of high self-esteem. They maintained that it was the ticket to good mental health (which had already started to deteriorate markedly), better behavior at home and school, and higher school achievement. Mind you, none of these claims had been subjected to anything remotely resembling the scientific method. They were snatched out of thin air by intellectually arrogant people who used the mystique of their titles and impressive capital letters after their names to convince the media and the public that everything they so snatched was the truth.

In fact, the idea that high self-esteem is a good thing is not the truth. Researchers using the scientific method have since discovered pretty much the opposite. For starters, high self-esteem does not lead to better mental health. People—children and teens included—who possess a high opinion of themselves and their abilities generally have poor coping skills. They are highly prone to episodes of depression. Why? Because the world rarely confirms that they are as great and wonderful as they think they are. Concerning their behavior, they tend to be manipulative (they think they are entitled; therefore, the end justifies the means), ungrateful (because they think they deserve whatever they receive), and unpleasant (especially when they don't get their way). And isn't it interesting that as parents and teachers have devoted more and more energy to promoting high self-esteem, measures of academic accomplishment have slid downhill? Turns out that people with inflated opinions of themselves believe anything they do is worthy of merit; therefore, they tend to do the minimum, if that. They're already wonderful! Why try harder?

The capital-letters-after-their-names people told parents and teachers that in order to instill high self-esteem, they had to do three things: first, they had to praise children a lot, for just about anything; second, they had to give kids lots of attention; third, they were to reward children for making even the smallest efforts. Turns out that praise and reward often backfire, that they are much less motivating than originally thought, and that they can, in certain situations, even reduce motivation. Giving children lots of attention has backfired as well. Attention is addictive. The more they get, the more they want, and the more obnoxious they become in their attempts to fill the ever-deepening hole that the addiction creates. Children who engage in lots of what is called "attention-seeking behavior" are not starved for it; they are addicted to it. They don't need more; they need less—much less.

In one of the exercises I often conduct with my audiences, I ask two questions:

1. "Raise your hand if you believe high self-esteem is a good thing and that responsible adults should do all they can to help children acquire it." (In the typical audience, at least 80 percent of hands go up.)
2. "Now raise your hand if, given a choice, you'd rather live next door to a person with high self-esteem as opposed to a person who is humble and modest." (No hands go up, and I point out that what they've just told me is that they want their kids to have high self-esteem but don't want to live next door to them when they grow up.)

Indeed, if the research is to be believed, people with high self-esteem do not make good neighbors. They possess a correspondingly low sense of social obligation. They are not service-minded. They want *you* to pay attention to and do things for *them*. Good neighbors do just the opposite: they pay attention and look for opportunities to serve. If you're sick, they offer to cut your grass and walk your dog. People with high self-esteem don't tend to do those sorts of things unless they are trying to obligate you to them—they tend, remember, to be manipulative.

"But John," I often hear, "I want my child to be confident. Isn't that what high self-esteem is all about?"

Well, that's interesting, because researchers have discovered that people with high self-esteem are indeed confident . . . overly so, in fact. They tend to overestimate their abilities. That leads not to high achievement but underachievement. Furthermore, people with high self-esteem tend to be handicapped by fears of failure. In the face of challenging circumstances, they are likely to cave in, drop out, or make excuses for themselves. Courage—the willingness to take on a task even when the risk of failure is high—and confidence are two entirely different things. I'll take courage over confidence any day.

It's no coincidence that this self-esteem claptrap wormed its way into America's parenting and educational cultures as secular humanist values were elbowing biblical values to the sidelines. Parents who reprimanded their children for acting too big for their britches, acting like they were the center of the universe, and riding high horses, were echoing the Bible, which clearly says that a high opinion of oneself and one's accomplishments is to be guarded against, that the proud will be brought low, and that humility is the center-piece of a properly outfitted character (see, for example, Proverbs 16:18; Philippians 2:5-8; James 4:6).

For children to stop celebrating themselves, adults need to stop celebrating children, making idols of them. Parents need to stop bragging about their children's accomplishments as if having a high-achieving child is proof of being a high-achieving parent. A fitting first step is for parents to not plas-ter their cars with stickers proclaiming that their children are honor students or "terrific kids." A second step is for parents, when they get together, to not talk about their children's accomplishments. All this bragging is unbecoming. It's insecure, as if parents' status in life is defined by their children's successes.

It would go a long way toward putting American parenting back on track if parents would again begin using the reprimands I heard when I was young. Then maybe we could get on with the business of raising good neighbors (the subject of the next chapter).

The Bible Tells Me So!

Those who exalt themselves will be humbled, and those who humble themselves will be exalted.

—MATTHEW 23:12, NIV

Jesus is the perfect model of humility. He came to serve, not to be served (see Matthew 20:28). As Paul says, "He made himself nothing by taking the very nature of a servant, being made in human likeness" (Philippians 2:7, NIV). Parents who want their children to develop a Christlike nature need to train them "in the way [they] should go" (Proverbs 22:6). That means training in humility—in putting on a servant's nature—should start early.

To Ponder and Discuss

Do you want your children to eventually develop Christlike attitudes toward themselves, their proper place in life, and their responsibilities toward others? If the answer is yes, do you think you've started them out on the right path? Are there times when you treat your children as if they were idols? What can you begin doing today to better help them develop a servant's heart?

11

"Good Citizenship Begins at Home"

Pre–1960s parents intuitively understood that proper parenting was an act of love for their neighbors—that the parents' foremost obligation was to the community and, by extension, the culture. Their purpose, therefore, was to produce good citizens and good neighbors—individuals who would strengthen America and make it a better place. This was accomplished by training children in proper moral and ethical values, including respect for others regardless of their station in life; an unconditional willingness to take initiative and take on responsibility even to the point of self-sacrifice; trustworthiness, compassion, cooperative obedience to legitimate authority; and a predisposition toward doing their best no matter the challenge. These values were historically unique. Forged during the Colonial and Revolutionary periods, they distinguished America from its European cousins.

The "Greatest Generation"—composed of Americans who grew into adulthood during the years encompassing the Great Depression and World War II (1929–1945)—was the last generation to subscribe to this child-rearing ethic. As a rule, the people of this generation were patriots who believed America was the greatest nation ever founded and strove to transmit its distinctive values to their children. Through no fault of these parents, their children—the Baby Boomers—failed to carry this torch forward. By the time the Boomers began having children, America had become a postmodern, progressive culture that had embraced individualism, a philosophy that prioritizes the individual's goals and desires above those of society and stresses the individual's right to create his or her own identity. This freedom is not, by a long shot, the same freedom embodied in the Declaration of Independence; rather, it is a do-your-own-thing hedonism—that is, self-indulgence. Take it from someone who subscribed to this seductive philosophy during his early adulthood: individualism is corrosive, destructive, and antithetical to all of the values held dear by our forefathers and foremothers. The bohemian, hippie, and yippie movements of the 1950s, 1960s, and 1970s, respectively—all of which flaunted disdain for traditional American values—were individualism's offspring.

America's mental health establishment—the curator of

postmodern progressivism—embraced individualism and began beating the drum of self-esteem, proclaiming that feeling good about oneself was the centerpiece of a life well lived. The typical reader may think this concept has been around forever—it has, after all, become as "American" as Mom, the flag, and apple pie—when in fact it did not enter the vernacular until the late 1960s. Around the same time, child rearing became *parenting*, a term that reflected a radical new set of understandings, central to which was the belief that a parent's foremost responsibility was not to train future citizens in traditional American values (which were also biblical values) but instead to instill high self-esteem. In a blink of America's eye, the family shifted from being adult- or marriage-centered to being child-centered. Children became Big Deals, and meeting their supposed "needs"—which are not *needs* at all but various entitlements—became parenting's primary objective.

Thus, there are several notable differences between the child rearing of yesteryear and post–1960s parenting:

1. Traditional child rearing was not "all about" the child. Parents felt obligation to their children, of course, but they felt a larger obligation to their neighbors, their children's teachers, the community, and the culture. Today's parents, by and large, seem to feel obligation only to their children.
2. Parents of yesteryear were not much concerned with their children's accomplishments, including their grades. They insisted that their children always do

their best, but if they were capable of only Cs along with occasional Bs, their parents were unlikely to do much, if anything, to artificially inflate grades. Today's parents, by contrast, will go to great lengths to promote and increase their children's skills and, therefore, their athletic and academic accomplishments.

3. Parents of yesteryear were proud of but did not tout their children's accomplishments. A 1950s parent who bragged about her children's accomplishments or talked incessantly about all the marvelous things she was doing for her kids would have been regarded by her peers as somewhat odd, even boorish. Many of today's parents talk about their children almost obsessively and even put bumper stickers on their cars proclaiming that their children are honor students, on championship teams, attend top-notch universities ("Harvard Parent!"), and are, at the very least, "terrific."

Parents of yesteryear saw their children through wide-angle lenses that enabled proper perspective. Children were little fish in a big pond. Today's parents, by contrast, tend to be afflicted with parenting tunnel vision, and the entire visual field at the end of the tunnel is occupied by the children. Their children are Big Fish at the center of a pond that exists to advance and fulfill the children's "needs." This overfocus on children has unfortunate consequences for all concerned.

It increases stress for parents (mothers especially), promotes self-centeredness in children, and, because the entire adult community is not pulling together as it once did, elevates the likelihood of conflict between parents and other adults in the community. The more contact an adult has with a child, the greater the likelihood of conflict, which is why teachers complain to me so often that when they discipline children, parents complain, sometimes threateningly.

The fault in all of this, mind you, is not with the parents. The fault lies in the fact that since the 1960s, individualism has been ascendant and good citizenship has been on the wane. The (supposed) needs of the almighty Self have trumped any larger, communitarian concerns. Parents have simply been swept up and carried along by social forces that are at best difficult to resist. Unfortunately, the end result is that children have become idols of a sort—put on pedestals, pampered, and protected from responsibilities and realities that strengthen not only children but communities and culture as well. Responsibilities like chores, for example.

Citizen Child

In America, ideal citizens are and have always been defined to a significant degree by their willingness to serve others without promise of compensation—to do for others or take on a civic project simply because it needs to be done. America has more volunteer organizations per capita than any other nation on the planet. Volunteerism is not a defining feature of countries that have embraced big government or have had big government forced upon them. Big Nanny doesn't encourage volunteerism. Volunteers, after all, might come up with their own ideas concerning how things ought to be done, ideas that are not in keeping with Big Nanny's big plans. In other words, for America to remain a vital republic in which government is held to a minimum, volunteerism must thrive. For it to thrive requires that parents raise children who are service minded and actively responsible, compassionate citizens who are willing to do for others without condition.

Most people born before the birth of the welfare state in the late 1960s (the so-called Great Society)—myself included—grew up with family responsibilities: chores. From the time we were able to pitch in, we pitched in. Our chores, which involved work in and around the house, took precedence over just about anything else. "First you do what you *have* to do, then you can do what you *want* to do" was Grandma's rule. In many cases, chores had to be done first thing upon coming home from school, even before homework.

I am a member of the last generation of children who were told that their friends could come out and play only when they had finished their chores. I remember a friend's mom telling me that if I sat on their front porch and my friend knew I was waiting, "maybe he'll get a move on." And if we ever were so bold as to complain about our chores, we were likely told, "You eat; therefore, you work." And that was that. You consumed; therefore, you contributed to the extent you were capable of making a contribution. "Good citizenship begins in the home," we were told. As is the case with America, a family's strength derives in significant part from the fact that all of its members pull together.

Before my fourth birthday, my mother, a single parent at the time, taught me to wash floors. There's a photo of me doing so that Mom took with her Brownie camera. If you flip it over, the date indicates I was not yet four.

"Did you set this up, Mom?" I asked when I came across it.

"Land sakes, no," she answered. "You were washing floors by then. You rather enjoyed it, as I remember. Used to ask me if you could."

Did I wash floors as well as my mother could have? Not a chance. But that was not the point of the exercise. Rather, Mom taught me to wash floors in order to teach me that something cannot be had for nothing, all relationships are give-and-take, and good citizenship begins in the home. These were values she wanted to instill in me. Where my chores were concerned, she always held me to reasonable standards, but there was never any question whether she could have done them better and faster than I did. In fact, she did not hesitate to point out to me when I missed a spot on the floor or left some weeds unpulled in the garden.

A mother once asked me, "What chores are developmentally appropriate for a three-and-a-half-year-old girl?"

That's the way parents talk when they've read too many parenting books and magazine articles. The question implies there might be a body of research that has identified age-appropriate (and perhaps even gender-appropriate) chores so that parents will not make the dreaded mistake of assigning chores that might prove traumatic, and the thus-traumatized child may never recover from the experience. Needless to say, the child's self-esteem will be trashed.

"Teach her to wash floors," I said nonchalantly.

She stared at me incredulously for several seconds. "Don't you think washing floors is a bit much for a three-year-old?"

"My mother didn't think so," I replied. "I strongly encourage you to go home and begin teaching your daughter what a competent little person she is. Now's the ideal time to be doing so, but time's a-wastin'."

Three-year-olds love to imitate adults. This is the age at which kids begin wanting to dress up in adult clothes and fantasize playing various adult roles. Threes will often invent imaginary playmates that they can play at being adults with. At this age, children will also imitate their parents when they are working at something around the house. If one of their parents is cleaning, they want to clean too. If their parents are working in the yard, they want to work in the yard too. This is the ideal age to be assigning regular chores to a child. When parents don't capitalize on the natural desire of the three-year-old to pitch in and help around the house, the desire fades away. The older child is more likely to resist doing chores—to complain, do them halfheartedly, or even downright refuse.

I doubt that the above mom went home and put her three-year-old daughter to work washing floors. She didn't look pleased with my answer. Turn her daughter into household help? No way! Maybe I could have told her that according to research done at several Ivy League institutions, it would be developmentally appropriate and not at all traumatic for her to have her daughter tell her when the dog's bowl needed more water. That's what a mother once told me was her five-year-old daughter's chore (with emphasis on the singular): tell her when the dog's water bowl needed filling. Telling a mother when she needs to perform a chore is now a chore. What a concept!

Before I was five, my mother taught me to wash my own clothes in her washing "machine"—a galvanized tub onto which she had bolted hand rollers. If memory serves me well, she did not have a washboard. I learned to wash clothes in the down-by-the-river fashion: on my knees, pulling two hand-fuls of clothing out of the sudsy water and rubbing them together where there was a stain.

Someone once asked me how Mom got me to do these things. What did she reward me with? Ha! She rewarded me with nothing. The reward was in doing a good job, which she told me I'd done, but only when I'd actually done so. If, on the other hand, I had not done a good job, she pointed that out too and made me correct my lapse. She got me to do things like washing floors and washing clothes by telling me I was going to do them.

Maybe she said, "John Rosemond, you look like you're at wit's end with nothing to do. Well, I've got something for you to do then. You come with me."

In any case, that was that. Mom employed neither entice-ments nor threats of punishment, just straightforward, plain talk, which is how parents should give instructions in the first place. Plain talk results in plain action. The more words one uses when giving instructions to children, the more it sounds like persuasion, in which case children will act like they are not persuaded and therefore push back in one way, shape, or form.

That brings up the issue of how much money children should be paid for doing chores. The answer is nothing. They are already being compensated, and richly so. They are being fed, clothed, sheltered, transported, educated, provided good medical care, taken on vacations, given toys and various electronic devices, and most important of all, protected from the ravages of wild animals, all at no cost to them whatsoever. Besides, paying children for chores is likely to create the impression that if they do not need money that week, they are under no requirement to do their chores.

"Are you against allowances?" a parent might ask.

Not at all, but an allowance should be given with one hand and chores with the other, and never should the two hands be rubbed together. Do not mix the two issues, in other words. An allowance should represent some degree of fiscal responsibility that parents have transferred to children. With said money, for example, the children are now responsible for purchasing their own recreation unless it involves at least one other family member. That's just a "for example," mind you. The point is, I do not believe allowances should be free money.

My wife and I assigned chores to our kids, and belatedly so, when they were ten and six years old. Up until then, they were on the "family welfare plan," meaning they got something for nothing. Good citizens do not expect something for nothing, so up until those ages, Willie and I will admit to not having taught our kids the basics of good citizenship. (I learned almost everything I know about children and how to raise 'em right through on-the-job training that involved lots of trial and error, with an emphasis on *error*.)

At ten and six, Eric and Amy began doing almost all of the housework. They each had a morning (or before school) chore, an after lunch (or after school) chore, and a chore that had to be done immediately after the evening meal. Three chores per day times two children times seven days equals forty-two chores! Needless to say, our house was always clean and tidy. This work took each child about forty-five minutes a day, *for which they were not paid*. At age thirteen, they each began to receive allowances along with certain fiscal responsibilities that forced them to set fiscal priorities, plan ahead, and budget.

When Willie and I unveiled the new Rosemond family chore plan to our kids, they stared at us like we'd lost our minds. Finally, Eric said, "What are you going to pay us?"

"Nothing," I said. "Let me point out that no one pays your mother for cooking supper or doing laundry, and no one pays me for cutting the grass."

"But none of our friends have to do all of this stuff around their houses," he replied, "and when they do, their parents pay them!"

"Which is why you should no longer tell me what other parents are doing and not doing, Eric."

"What do you mean?"

"I mean your mother and I have decided that from now on, we are going to be the weirdest parents in town."

Ten years later, Eric called us from college and said, "You know, there were times when I really resented that I wasn't being raised like other kids I knew, but I've been at college now for two years, and I'm beginning to understand why you did what you did. I am prepared in ways that lots of kids in my generation aren't, and it's because you guys did things so differently from the way other parents were doing things. Anyway, I'm calling just to say thanks."

Amy called to say the same thing when she was in college. Both of the kids are reasonably intelligent, but neither is intellectually gifted. Neither possesses outstanding artistic or athletic skills. They did not go to top-tier universities (although they might defensively disagree), do not have high-status jobs, and are not wealthy and probably never will be. But they are good citizens who love America and are unconditionally willing to serve its best interests. And that's good enough for me.

The Bible Tells Me So!

I have shown you in every way, by laboring like this, that you must support the weak. And remember the words of the Lord Jesus, that He said, "It is more blessed to give than to receive."

—*ACTS 20:35*

Now abide faith, hope, love, these three; but the greatest of these is love.
—*1 CORINTHIANS 13:13*

Our citizenship is in heaven, and from it we await a Savior, the Lord Jesus Christ.
—*PHILIPPIANS 3:20, ESV*

Preparing children for citizenship in heaven involves guiding them in developing a servant's heart toward their fellow earthly citizens. Teach the virtues of charity, community service, and humility through example and assignment.

To Ponder and Discuss

Has the primary purpose of your child rearing been to raise good citizens who love America and would be willing to make sacrifices in its defense? If not, what has your purpose been? Are your children responsible citizens of your family? If not, why not? What chores can they begin doing today?

12

"Count Your Blessings"

Largely because they think life should be fair, children tend to complain a lot. In fact, whenever you encounter adults who complain a lot about the many inequities and injustices that have beset their lives or the bad hand of cards they've been dealt, you can bet you have encountered adults who are still, emotionally and intellectually, children.

One way human beings avoid accepting responsibility for their lot in life or deny they are at all responsible for it is by complaining. Complainers are self-anointed victims. The villains in their lives are mostly other adults, but sometimes these very immature folks are victims of such impersonal things as the weather, traffic, mathematics (things just don't add up), gravity, the length of the day, the condition of the roads, and so on.

Reading the account of mankind's fall in Genesis 3, you can almost hear the whining tone of Adam's and then Eve's denial of responsibility for having eaten the fruit of the tree of knowledge. "Don't blame me!" they each complain. "It's not my fault!" (After passing the buck to Eve, Adam even tells God, "You gave her to me!" Complaining and buck-passing have been around for a long time.)

One of the hurdles that separates childhood from authentic adulthood is accepting responsibility for your lot in life along with accepting that, in the final analysis, the only person who can alter your lot in life is you. Some people never clear this hurdle. You likely know some of these people. They don't know this about themselves, however. Self-anointed victimhood and self-insight are incompatible.

Some time back, Willie and I were conversing with a woman we'd just met. She told us, rather proudly, that she absolutely, unequivocally rejected the role of victim. Her life, she said, was definitely not a drama. Not less than five minutes later, she launched into a description of her family's ongoing, multigenerational soap opera in which certain family members were always doing bad things to other family members—she being one of the latter. Her obvious inability to see that she was indeed one of the self-anointed victims she denied being was amazing, really. As Grandma would have said, "She can't see past the end of her own nose."

To employ another popular metaphor, authentic adults see the proverbial glass as half full while perpetual children tend to see it as half empty. It's hard to satisfy a child, and the more one tries to satisfy a child, the harder it becomes. One of the most important parenting tasks is helping children to see the glass as half full. So when children complained, Grandma would say, "Count your blessings."

If my experience was typical, then when an adult tells complaining children to count their blessings—to take notice of the good things in and about their lives—their reaction is "*What?*" Like being told that when all of their trophies and good grades have been counted and catalogued, people are really just little fish in a big pond or that "being really smart and a dollar will get you a cup of coffee" (another of Grandma's sprightly aphorisms), children do not comprehend. At that moment, after all, they are under victimhood's evil sway. They can't see past the ends of their own noses. They've got potatoes in their ears. They're going to have to learn their lessons the hard way.

A mother once told me that she sent her complaining eight-year-old son to his room with instructions that he could not come out until he had written down ten things he should be thankful for. It took him four hours. That's a child for you. It would take authentic adults ten minutes—and only if they wrote slowly. That's the difference between children (of whatever age) and genuine people who have earned the title of adult. Children count the negatives in their lives; adults count their blessings.

Here's how to grow ungrateful children: give them a lot. The more children are given, the less grateful they are. Ken Blanchard, the author of *Lead Like Jesus*, says that children are born with "selfish hearts." Indeed, and the more they are given and the more they have, the more selfish their hearts become. This is one of the lessons to be gleaned from the story of the rich man who asked Jesus what he had to do to attain eternal life. Jesus told him to sell all of his possessions and follow him. The rich man was unable to part from his wealth, and Jesus commented that it is easier for a camel to pass through the eye of a needle than for a rich man to enter the Kingdom of God (see Matthew 19:16-30).

Children who have everything they've ever asked for are like that rich man. They've become addicted to getting, and the more they get, the more they want, and the more selfish and demanding and ungrateful and complaining they become. When people think of idolaters, they tend to think of adults, but children make idols of things as well, and their idolatry is as spiritually hobbling as idolatry in an adult—more so, in fact, because the earlier in a person's life that idolatry gets its grip, the harder it is for the person to ever shake loose of it.

The old parenting aphorisms "Count your blessings" and "You're going to have to stew in your own juices about this" are joined at the hip. Put together they become "If you don't start counting your blessings, then I'm just going to let you stew in your own juices." In other words, the solution to complaining is to count your blessings, and it is your choice whether to be grateful or stew in misery. Grandma wasn't going to solve the problem, whatever it was. Effectively, both aphorisms said, "You've come to the wrong person with this, kiddo. I'm not going to become a player in your personal soap opera."

I think my generation, the early Baby Boomers (those born before 1955), is the last reasonably sturdy American generation (but we were not, by a long shot, as sturdy as our parents' generation). By and large, we looked forward to leaving home and being on our own. By and large, we took and take responsibility for our lives. Polls consistently reveal that my peers vote for politicians who represent and promote personal responsibility. The younger the person, the more likely it is that he or she will vote for politicians who promise entitlements. To us, rejecting handouts is a matter of personal pride (by the way, Social Security and Medicare are not entitlements—we've paid for them). We learned early on to size ourselves to our britches, to stew in our own juices, and to count our blessings. That's how we learned, eventually, to stand on our own two feet.

In other words, these things Grandma said are the stuff of personal sturdiness. As such, they are the stuff of sturdy marriages, sturdy communities, and a sturdy nation. Truly, America is strengthened by citizens who count their blessings. More important, God is honored by people who count their blessings, because all blessings come from him.

Give thanks, children, give thanks.

The Bible Tells Me So!

Be filled with the Spirit . . . giving thanks always for all things to God the Father in the name of our Lord Jesus Christ.

—EPHESIANS 5:18, 20

Let the peace of Christ rule in your hearts, to which indeed you were called in one body. And be thankful. Let the word of Christ dwell in you richly, teaching and admonishing one another in all wisdom, singing psalms and hymns and spiritual songs, with thankfulness in your hearts to God. And whatever you do, in word or deed, do everything in the name of the Lord Jesus, giving thanks to God the Father through him.

—COLOSSIANS 3:15-17, ESV

Thankfulness and gratefulness for the blessings in one's life, even the blessings of trouble and trial, are ways of honoring God, who made *all* things. Teach your children to be grateful for what they have instead of dwelling on what they do not have.

To Ponder and Discuss

Would you describe your children as more grateful than ungrateful, or the other way around? Do they seem to have an entitlement mentality, meaning they are never satisfied, always want more, and lack gratefulness? Do they take for granted the good life they lead? If so, how might you have unwittingly, with good intentions, contributed to that attitude? What can you begin doing today to help them turn that self-destructive attitude around?

13

"You Can't Hoodoo the Hoodoo Man"

Grandma probably never told her kids, "You can't hoodoo the Hoodoo Man." I did, though. The so-called Hoodoo Man/Hoodoo Woman was what blacks in the Deep South, way back when, called someone who either was a con artist or had special, secret knowledge. The knowledge in question was usually of the evil sort. The Hoodoo Man/Woman knew how to use charms to accomplish certain things—to make someone fall in love with someone else, to put a curse on someone, or to cause someone to become ill.

Children think they can fool adults. Some children are more convinced of this than others. Some have even discovered they *can* fool adults. Those are very clever children indeed. My children discovered early on that they couldn't fool me. I was the Hoodoo Man in their lives. I was able to occupy this role because I had been a very clever child who had often been able to fool adults. As a child, I was quite proud of my ability to con adults into believing my lies. I had no idea what a liability it was to be a good liar. The more I got away with lies, the more bad things I did, thinking that if I was caught, I could lie my way out of trouble. Unfortunately, I carried this ball and chain into adulthood, where I eventually discovered that I wasn't that clever after all. Courtesy of my own background, I am able to see through clever people rather quickly. I don't like them. I want to get away from them as quickly as I can, perhaps because they remind me of my former self, which still stands off in the shadows, beckoning. If it weren't for Christ Jesus, I'd still be clever.

As a consequence of my personal experience with being clever, I was determined from early on in my kids' lives not to let them go down that road. So, I became the former Hoodoo Man whom they couldn't hoodoo.

Tales of Hoodoo

When Eric was about eight and his sister was four, he came to me one day and told me that Amy had taken something out of his room. She had been asking him to let her play with it, and he wouldn't let her because it was one of his prized possessions. It was fragile, and he was afraid she'd break it. I told him to ask her for it.

"But Dad," he said, "she's just going to tell me she doesn't have it, and what do I do then?"

I agreed and told him I'd handle it, however reluctantly. I called out to Amy, and she appeared in front of me.

"Go get the (whatever it was) you took from Eric's room and give it to me," I said. That, by the way, is an example of "Ask them no questions and they'll tell you no lies" (see chapter 21). I did not ask her if she took it, because she would have lied for sure. Unfortunately, she lied anyway.

"I don't have it, Daddy," she said, trying to charm me with her oh-so-innocent blue eyes.

"Yes, Amy, you do. You asked Eric if you could play with it, and he said no. So you waited until he left his room, snuck in and took it, and hid it in your room. Now, go get it and give it to me, or I'm going to go in there and find it, and then you're going to be in lots of trouble."

Her innocence turned to malevolence. She glared up at me for a few seconds and then, emphasizing each word, she snarled, "How—did—you—know?"

And without missing a beat, I said, "I know *everything*!"

Her defiant expression turned to wide-eyed amazement. Without another word, she went into her room and emerged moments later with Eric's whatever-it-was in her hand. "I'm sorry," she said, handing it over to me.

The Hoodoo Man strikes again!

On a much later occasion, Eric and I were driving down the road together when he suddenly told me he wasn't going to get a good grade in English that grading period, which happened to be the first of his first year in junior high school—seventh grade, to be precise.

"What's that all about, Eric? You've always done well in English."

"Well, Dad," he said, "I don't know how to explain this to you, exactly, other than to just say my English teacher doesn't like me."

"She doesn't like you?"

"No, Dad, she doesn't like me. I turn in my best work, and she marks all over it in red. She blames me for things I haven't done. She even mocks my answers when I raise my hand! I do my best in her class, Dad—really, I do—but I just can't satisfy her. She doesn't like me, Dad, so don't expect more than a C in English this grading period."

"I see," I said. "Let me ask you something. How many kids are there in that class? An estimate, you know."

"Uh, I really don't know, Dad. Maybe thirty."

"Am I to understand that she doesn't like any of them?"

"No, Dad," he said. "She just doesn't like me and one other guy."

"I see. That's very interesting." And I just kept on driving, my eyes on the road.

After maybe thirty seconds had gone by—which, as you know, is a long time in a conversation—Eric said, "Dad?"

"Yes?"

"You're not saying anything. You're making me kind of nervous."

"Nervous? I'm making you nervous?"

"Yeah, Dad, it's like you're thinking something but aren't saying it."

"You want to hear what I'm thinking?"

"I mean, yeah, I want to hear it. What are you thinking?"

"I'm thinking you can't hoodoo the Hoodoo Man."

"What do you mean by that, Dad?"

"I mean what I've told you before, Eric. You can't fool me. I know what's going on in that English class."

"You do?" he said, a slight tremor in his voice.

"Yep, I do. You're a troublemaker. You and one other guy are making it difficult for your English teacher to do her job. You probably think you're funny. And now that you realize your report card grade in English is not going to be up to standards, you're trying to blow smoke all over the problem, trying to fool me. Well, Eric, you can't hoodoo the Hoodoo Man. I know what you're doing in her class, and I know what you're trying to do right now, and I have but one thing to tell you. If you don't get at least a B in her class, you are going to be grounded for the entire next grading period. And if you don't get a B in her class when that grounding is over, then there'll be another one."

"Dad! You're kidding!"

Still keeping my eyes on the road, I said, "Nope."

"But how am I going to get a B? There are only three weeks left, and I'm making a C right now. Maybe even a D! I can't make a B! Not now!"

"Then you're going to be grounded for an entire grading period, so you better figure out how to make that B. Wash her car, clean her classroom after school, ask her for extra work, cut her grass on the weekend, walk her dog. You better figure it out. Oh, and before you say anything else, this conversation is now officially over."

"But Dad!"

"Over."

He made a B in her class. I don't know what he did to bring his grade up to a B. I never even asked. What I do know is that whatever he did had a lot to do with the Hoodoo Man. Sometimes, as it turns out, a father can do certain things to at least lessen the possibility that his sins will be visited upon his kids.

The Bible Tells Me So!

Once again, the Bible story that comes to mind is Western civilization's first parenting story: the story of Adam and Eve told in Genesis 3. One of its lessons is that parents who know their children well—and who knows his children better than God?—ought to know when their children are trying to pull one over on them, when they're trying to pull some hoodoo. You may recall that after informing Adam of the one rule and then creating Eve, God wanders off. When he reenters, stage right, he immediately notices they are trying to hide something from him. And he accepts no ifs, ands, or buts. (He was obviously Grandma's role model.)

I used to tell my kids, "I know you better than you know

yourself because I've known you from before your awareness of yourself awakened, so do yourself, and me, a favor and don't try to put something over on me." Nonetheless, every so often I had to remind them of my amazing ability to see right through them.

To Ponder and Discuss

It's certainly tempting to give one's own kids the benefit of the doubt, but there are times when kids benefit from being doubted. Have you allowed your kids to scam you—to pull a hoodoo on you? What is it that causes you not to see their faults clearly?

14

"Money Doesn't Grow on Trees"

Even as a child, I was a realist. For example, I never really believed in Santa Claus or the tooth fairy, and I never thought there was a pot of gold waiting for me if I could locate the elusive end of a rainbow. I never thought money grew on trees, either. Nonetheless, on more than a few occasions my parents felt the need to inform me that money trees did not exist. It was the sort of thing that I had no reply to, other than perhaps a resigned "I know." It ended the conversation, if conversation was even the appropriate word. More often than not, the "conversation" went something like this:

"Dad," I asked, "can I have two dollars to go to the movies with my friends?"

"Do you think money grows on trees?"

"No."

"Right. No."

"So can I?"

"I just told you. No."

"Why?"

"Y is a crooked letter."

"What does that mean?"

"I have no idea. My father said it to me. I'm just passing it along."

Those sorts of minimalistic exchanges were pretty much the norm in parent-child relationships back then. Grandma often talked like one might imagine the Neanderthals did. Grunt, grunt, grunt, period, end of conversation. Her generation may have been the Greatest Generation, but they were not always the Greatest Communicators—not with their kids, at least.

My parents were trying to teach me the virtue of being thrifty, of not letting oneself be seduced by what is currently called "eye candy"—stuff with great visual appeal but little, if any, long-term value. Actually, along with most members of their generation, they could have done a better job of explaining what they meant by asking us if we thought money was tree fruit. Sometimes, and this is one of those times, they said very little to a fault. Perhaps they thought their own example would be enough.

When each of our kids entered their teen years, Willie and I began giving them a monthly clothing and entertainment allowance. It was calculated based on estimates of how much we would be spending per month on clothing and entertainment for them. When we arrived at a figure, we cut it by 20 percent, and that became each child's monthly allowance.

As I said in chapter 11, I do not believe in simply giving children money. That sort of allowance is an entitlement that has no instructional value. It's simply money children can spend as the impulse moves them. The plan we used had great instructional value. Since we made it clear that we would not under any circumstances give any advances, the system forced them to budget, plan ahead, restrain impulse buying, and put money away for "rainy days." We also made it perfectly clear that should one of them bounce a check (the checking accounts we set up for them had no overdraft protection), the bank and merchant fines, plus a fifty dollar fine to us, would come out of the following month's allowance.

If proof is found in the pudding, so to speak, then the plan worked beautifully. Neither child ever bounced a check, and both learned, as young teenagers, how to budget money and plan for unanticipated expenses. As adults they are both excellent money managers.

It should go without saying that the earlier a child learns how to manage and stretch a dollar, the better. I have to believe that the "boomerang child" phenomenon is due in large part to kids who have not learned, prior to emancipation, the need to restrain their impulses when it comes to spending. As Grandma might have said, borrowing from another of her favorite sayings, their eyes are bigger than their wallets.

The Bible Tells Me So!

Keep your life free from love of money, and be content with what you have, for he has said, "I will never leave you nor forsake you."
—HEBREWS 13:5, ESV

For the love of money is a root of all kinds of evils. It is through this craving that some have wandered away from the faith and pierced themselves with many pangs.
—1 TIMOTHY 6:10, ESV

No one can serve two masters, for either he will hate the one and love the other, or he will be devoted to the one and despise the other. You cannot serve God and money.
—MATTHEW 6:24, ESV

He who loves money will not be satisfied with money, nor he who loves wealth with his income; this also is vanity.
—ECCLESIASTES 5:10, ESV

God wants parents to teach their children to be frugal, to not love money. The Bible is perfectly clear on that point. But as with most things, frugality can become an idol, an end in itself. Carried past a certain point, frugality is just another form of love of money. People who take great pride in their frugality to the point of making a public display of it are really no different from the Pharisees who made public displays of their religiosity.

To Ponder and Discuss

Do your kids seem to think that money grows on trees? Where did they ever get that idea? What specific steps can you take that will help them realize that money is not an entitlement and should not be spent on frivolous things?

15

"I'm Only Going to Say This Once"

This chapter comes to you courtesy of an anonymous mother I saw attempting to discipline her young son (I estimated his age at five) in a crowded store in eastern North Carolina on December 23, 2014.

I was browsing through a sale table of blue jeans when I heard a mother bark, "Stop it!"

I turned around, as did everyone else within earshot. Mother and child were about twenty feet away, in front of another clothing display. She was glaring threateningly in his direction. He must not have taken her seriously because she barked it again, only louder.

"Stop it! You'd better stop it right now or you're going to be in trouble!"

I don't know what the boy was doing because the display hid him from view. He was probably handling the clothes. Children, especially boys, touch things. Boys are tactile. They grow up to be men who are tactile and want to handle tools and engines and other mechanical stuff. Girls look. Boys touch. Whenever you hear a parent speaking loudly to a child in a store, there's a seven-in-ten chance the child is male.

"Jeremy! Did you hear me? I told you to stop! Now stop! Do you want me to take you outside?"

At this point, said agitated mother has told Jeremy (not his real name, of course) five times to stop doing whatever he was doing. I had turned back around by this point because I'd witnessed this sort of parent-child altercation many times. This was same-old, same-old. By the time things settled down, mom had told Jeremy to stop three more times and threatened him with trouble of some unspecified sort twice more. Actually, from all that I could gather, Jeremy didn't ever stop. Mom finally grabbed him and pulled him away from the stack of clothes in which he was exercising his tactile inclinations.

Jeremy's mother is the sort of mom who tells me her child is "very strong willed," doesn't listen to anything she says, and is driving her slowly bananas (or up a wall). The moms in question never realize they're telling me more—much more—about themselves than they are about their children. First, *all* children are strong willed. Some are blatant about it. Others are clever, devious, and underhanded about it. The former attract lots of attention to themselves. They are the ones whose parents call them strong willed. Second, all *adults* are strong willed too. You want things your way, don't you? Of course you do! (A woman once told me that no, she didn't want things her way; she wanted things God's way. That's very sweet, but she was really telling me that she just expresses her strong-willed nature in clever rather than obvious ways.) You want things your way, I want things my way—*all* of God's children want things their way! That is nothing more and nothing less than human nature. When paradise is restored, we will act at all times and in all ways according to God's will. In the meantime, we want things our way (more often than not). Third, today's parents use the term "strong willed" as a euphemism for disobedient. Fourth, whereas disobedience is the natural state of human affairs (see Genesis 3), parents who understand how to discipline can and will train their children to obey by the time said kids are three years old. In the 1950s and before, obedience by age three was the norm. That was before parents stopped telling children once and once only.

Going back to Jeremy: What reason does he have to take his mother seriously? Answer: none. His mother is nothing but, well, a windbag. She's a prime example of how windbags attempt to discipline their children: "Stop stop stop stop stop did you hear me if I have to say it one more time you're going to be in trouble did you hear me you'd better stop or there's going to be trouble stop I said what do I have to do to make you listen to me stop stop stop okay you're not going to be able to watch your program this afternoon if you don't stop do you want me to take you outside stop I said stop. . . ."

This sort of parent always reminds me of one of my favorite *The Far Side* cartoons. In the first frame, titled "What We Say to Dogs," a man is reprimanding his dog, saying, "Okay, Ginger! I've had it! You stay out of the garbage! Understand, Ginger? You stay out of the garbage, or else!" The second frame is titled "What They Hear," which is "Blah blah GINGER blah blah blah blah blah blah blah blah GINGER blah blah blah blah blah." Substitute "Jeremy" for "Ginger," and nothing changes. All Jeremy hears is "blah blah blah." He has no reason to listen. He has no reason to obey. Not because he's strong willed or some such thing, but because his mother and all too many of today's parents are windbags. They talk, talk, talk, talk, talk, but it is only on the extremely rare occasion that they act, and it is rarer still that they act effectively.

A few paragraphs back, I said that parents who understand how to discipline can and will train their children to obey by the time said kids are three years old. The primary feature of the discipline in question is the "I only tell you once" principle. Children pay attention when they've learned that their parents only say things once. When parents say things more than once, they unwittingly train their kids to be inattentive—to develop, over time, attention deficit disorder.

Over the years, lots and lots of parents have asked me, "How many times should I have to say something to my (fill in an age)-year-old before I can reasonably expect him/her to obey me?" I have a job because of parents such as these. Today, unlike sixty years ago, they are legion. The ubiquity of the question explains why today's parents are having so much more difficulty in the area of discipline than did their grandparents, great-grandparents, great-great-grandparents, and so on. That one question explains why I decided to write this book. I will venture to say that not one parent prior to 1960 asked that question. Having done most of my growing up prior to 1960, I don't think that's a stretch. Today's parents ask it because the pre–1960s parenting point of view has been all but lost.

Back then, children did not have attention deficit disorder. I'm serious. There is absolutely no evidence that this supposedly gene-based disorder was in noticeable evidence prior to the 1960s. That's why many, many teachers of that era were easily and successfully teaching elementary classes of forty-plus children. And by the way, the *plus* in the previous sentence goes all the way up to at least ninety-five, which is the number of first graders a woman told me she taught in one classroom by herself in the mid-1950s. She told me she had hardly any discipline problems.

What? You don't believe me? In third-world schools today, one often finds more than one hundred children being easily and successfully taught by one teacher. In 2014, a missionary to Africa told me that most one-room schoolhouses feature one teacher teaching more than one hundred children. "In all the time I was there," she said, "I only saw one discipline problem." When children come to school having already been taught that adults say things one time and one time only, one teacher can easily teach ninety-five or more children. Proof, both past and present, abounds.

Parents train children to pay attention and obey. Such training consists of two understandings:

1. The parents give instructions once and once only.
2. If and when the child does not carry out an instruction upon being told once and once only, parents issue memorable consequences. They do not fool around when it comes to that.

It's quite simple, really.

Now, does adopting a policy of telling children once and once only guarantee instant obedience 100 percent of the time? No, it doesn't. Remember, I told you earlier that the inclination toward disobedience is built into children. Obedience must be trained. But whereas that training can and should result in relative obedience by age three, even the most effective training will not result in 100 percent obedience by age three . . . or four . . . or ten . . . or even eighteen. In my experience, you can reasonably expect 70 percent by age three, 80 percent by age four, 90 percent by age ten, and 95 percent by age eighteen, at which point you send children off to college, the military, or full-time jobs that enable them to emancipate successfully by age twenty. Then the school of hard knocks takes over.

At this point, more than one reader is just dying to know how Jeremy's mother should have handled his tactile explorations in the store. The moment Jeremy began touching the clothing, she should have sacrificed her shopping, taken him by the hand, led him out of the store and to their car, taken him home, confined him to his room for the remainder of the day, and put him to bed immediately after supper.

"But, but John!" a reader is exclaiming. "You said to tell a child once! Didn't you leave out that Jeremy's mom should have told him, once, not to touch the stacks of clothing?"

Good question. Now, let me ask this question in return: How many times prior to December 23, 2014, do you think Jeremy's mom told him not to touch clothing and other things in stores? A dozen? Several dozen? Right! She has probably told him this same thing at least several dozen times. Jeremy's mom likely gave him the first of at least several dozen "don't touch" instructions two or three years ago. Ideally, that's when she should have acted. But she did not. She turned into a windbag, and she has been a windbag ever since. That is why five-year-old Jeremy did not pay any attention at all to his mother on December 23, 2014, in a large, crowded store in North Carolina.

And that is why I say that Jeremy's mom should never again tell him not to touch things in stores. She long ago went past the point of telling him once. From now on, she should simply act. If she never repeats herself again, and acts the very first time Jeremy crosses the line in a store, she will act calmly and purposefully. And Jeremy will begin to take her seriously, which is long overdue.

"But John!" the same reader exclaims. "You're saying that Jeremy's mother should stop her Christmas shopping and go home! That punishes her!"

That's correct, but she is punishing herself as it is. By doing what I just described, and doing it perhaps two or three more times, she will stop punishing herself. Because Jeremy will finally take her seriously, she will be able, finally, to take him into stores and have an enjoyable shopping experience. But yes, she will have to leave several shopping trips unfinished in order to make her point. Otherwise, she will be punishing herself in stores for who knows how many years to come.

Parents are forever asking me for discipline that does not inconvenience them in some way, however small. There is no such thing. Consider that the most inconvenienced people in a prison are the guards. They committed no crimes, yet when they're on the job, they're locked up with all sorts of bad, dangerous people. In short, there is no such thing as effective discipline that does not inconvenience, to one degree or another, the person—parent or teacher—who must enforce it.

Nothing is free, folks.

The Bible Tells Me So!

If you love me, you will keep my commandments.
—JOHN 14:15, ESV

One way we show our love for God is to obey him—to walk in his will and keep his commandments. Likewise, a child's obedience is a demonstration of love for his or her parents. The child, of course, does not see it that way. If you asked an obedient child, "Why do you obey your parents?" a young child—three to eight, approximately—would probably answer "Because they're my parents." An older child—nine to early adolescence—might give a more perceptive answer along the lines of "Because they love me." Nevertheless, without being able to articulate it, a child's obedience is an act of love.

Disobedience on the part of a child creates stress (expressed as anger, guilt, worry, and resentment) in the parent-child relationship. This stress interferes with the natural flow of affection between parent and child. Obedience on the part of the child reduces the need for discipline and eliminates the above emotional impediments (or prevents them from forming), thus releasing the full potential for mutual affection in the relationship.

Parents are children's first representation of God. It is their right to come to understand, courtesy of loving parents who exercise appropriate authority over them, that God is the source of ultimate love and ultimate authority.

To Ponder and Discuss

Are you like Jeremy's mom? Do you nag, nag, nag, nag, nag, and then nag some more, but rarely act? If so, can you identify one—just one—of your child's misbehaviors to which you can begin applying the "Say It Once!" principle? Don't bite off more than you can chew, and think your strategy through before you apply it. Then, begin experiencing the joy of eliminating behavior problems, one at a time.

16
"Lower the Boom!"

Similar in nature to giving children enough rope with which to hang themselves, the proverbial boom was "lowered" as somewhat of a last resort, after parents had applied various consequences to a child's misbehavior with no success. The boom in question was a *huge* consequence that had at least three figurative exclamation points after it. It was employed to get a child's attention, to emphasize that the parents had reached their limit, their last straw, concerning the misbehavior in question.

Let's face it: parents don't like to punish their kids. Well, there may in fact be the occasional sociopathic parent who does enjoy it, but normal, loving parents do not. (Besides which, sociopathic parents will not read this book, so it isn't necessary that I address them.) They simply realize that punishment is sometimes necessary. Hopefully, punishment reduces the likelihood that the misbehavior will occur again. That's a good thing, because the more a child misbehaves, the less happy the child is. Note that I used the word "hopefully." I did so because contrary to the prevailing myth, born of behavior modification theory, proper consequences properly applied do not guarantee that misbehavior will stop or even lessen. Humans are odd creatures. Animals, for example, are predictable. They are creatures of habit or instinct. Humans, however, are wont to do unpredictable things. One would predict that punishment makes misbehavior less likely, and sure enough, that's true of dogs and other animals. But where human beings are concerned, punishment can and sometimes does make misbehavior worse. Or it has no effect at all. So, punishment reduces the likelihood that a certain misbehavior will repeat itself . . . hopefully.

The second reason punishment is necessary has to do with the tendency of human beings to deny responsibility for bad things they do. This tendency has its beginning in the Garden of Eden. You may remember that when confronted by God with their transgression, both Adam and Eve attempted to pass the buck. Adam said Eve made him do it. He even implied it was God's fault for giving her to him. And then Eve said the serpent made her do it. Too bad—for us all. We can't be certain, but it is possible that had those two ancestors of ours confessed their sin and thrown themselves on God's mercy, he might have given them a reprieve. Oh well; that's for theologians to ponder. It was what it was, and things are what they are as a result. All children are like Adam and Eve. Their first inclination upon being busted for something bad they've done is to blame something or someone else.

Now, the fact is you cannot talk children into accepting responsibility for a misdeed. There are no magic words that will cause children to suddenly say, "Wow! That was brilliant, Mom! Your carefully chosen words have convinced me that it is better for me to confess to stealing the cookies from the cookie jar than to continue denying it. Thank you, Mom!" Precisely because no child in all of history has ever said words to that effect, punishment is necessary to assign responsibility that children won't willingly accept. Punishment is a means of slam-dunking children's often endless but-but-but-but-buting. Whether or not children will admit to wrongdoing, they are nonetheless going to have to experience the consequences of their wrongdoing.

Punishment is also a wake-up call. It puts children on notice that they're not fooling anyone and that if they know what's best, they will stop misbehaving before adults have to do something even worse to get them to wake up and smell the coffee. I've already gone over the fact that children have hard heads, thick skulls, and potatoes in their ears, and some kids have harder heads, thicker skulls, and more potatoes in their ears than others. In other words, some kids will wake up and smell the coffee in response to relatively small punishments; others require no less than BIG HUGE ENORMOUS GIGANTIC GARGANTUAN punishments before they will smell the coffee. (By the way, if you haven't noticed, some adults are like that too.) A BIG HUGE ENORMOUS GIGANTIC GARGANTUAN consequence is a boom—or, more accurately, a **BOOM!!!**

The reference is to a long pole that fixed the bottom of a sail to keep it from flapping around in the wind. A boom is a horizontal appendage to a mast. Some booms folded up when their ships were at rest, in harbor. When they were lowered, pity the poor seaman who was standing underneath. One experience with being underneath a boom as it was being lowered was enough to cause a wounded seaman to never make that mistake again. As it applies to children, the idiom refers to a punishment that will cause them to never misbehave in the same way again . . . theoretically, that is. Some children, after all, have heads so hard and skulls so thick that even the biggest, hugest, most enormous, gigantic, and gargantuan of punishments won't sink in. These kids are few and far between, but they're out there. As adults, they lose job after job (always blaming someone else for their misfortune), spend stretch after stretch in jail (always blaming someone else for their misfortune), and go through relationship after relationship (always blaming the other person). They just never learn. There aren't booms big and heavy enough to get through to them.

Don't worry, though. Your child is probably not one of them. Even if your child seems to have the thickest skull along with the hardest head God ever made, the likelihood is there's a boom big and heavy enough to get your child's attention. You just haven't found it yet. Or, more likely, you've been reluctant to use it. You've been unwilling to make your child really—I mean *really*—unhappy. So, the child keeps on misbehaving in the same ways, and you keep right on getting frustrated and angry and bent out of shape.

I said this earlier, but it bears repeating: when children do something bad, they need to feel bad about it. If you are the parent I just described, then when your children do bad things, *you* feel bad. That's upside down and backward. If you feel bad when your children misbehave, then your children do not feel bad, and feeling bad is what causes children to decide they're not going to misbehave in that fashion again. For your children's sake (remember, misbehavior diminishes happiness), you need to get over being reluctant to use a suitable boom the next time your children misbehave in some currently frustrating, aggravating, infuriating way.

One such boom is what I call "Kicking the Child Out of the Garden of Eden." When Adam and Eve transgressed and then each in turn tried to pass the buck, God knew they were going to need a lot of discipline. He also knew that the discipline they required was incompatible with life in Paradise. So he kicked them out, and their—and our—discipline began. (Thousands of years later, God is still at it, a testament to our hard heads, thick skulls, and ear potatoes.)

Kicking children out of the Garden means stripping them of all but the most basic and essential of possessions and privileges, and keeping them in this state of deprivation until they have repented of their errant ways and demonstrated their rehabilitation for a significant period of time.

Erin (not her real name, of course) was thirteen when her parents came to see me about her rebelliousness. She had always been strong willed, they said, but when she turned thirteen, it was as if a switch had been thrown. She became belligerently defiant and disrespectful—determined, it seemed, to prove to her parents that they had no control over her life whatsoever. She was certainly a master at pushing their buttons. She would ask them for something outrageous, they would say no, and she would go into a rage, sometimes lacing it with various obscenities that are not suitable to be printed in any book. Her mother would begin crying, which never failed to cause her father to go into a rage of his own. Then, in the typical scenario, Erin would run out of the house, screaming that she was never coming back, and her parents would spend the rest of the day and maybe even that night and part of the next day trying to figure out at which of her friends' houses she had sought refuge. I figured Erin was simply rehearsing for the reality television show she was eventually going to create.

Erin's parents were fairly well off, so Erin enjoyed a better-than-good standard of living. She had lots of nice clothes and possessions. Ripe for the kicking, she was. Her parents went home from their first appointment with me, and while Erin was at school, they stripped her room down to bare essentials. They confiscated her favorite clothes and all of her favorite stuff, including her computer. Then they called their cell phone provider and shut off Erin's number. When Erin came home, her parents told her she was going to live in that state of deprivation until she had managed to go a full month without one episode of tantrum, obscenity, disobedience, or disrespect. If, during the first month, she had an episode, her required month would begin anew the next day. As predicted, Erin had a meltdown. She raged and disrespected quite loudly for quite some time, throwing in lots of obscenities for good measure, then ran out of the house saying she was never coming back. Her parents and I had discussed that possibility. I had recommended letting her go.

"Give her an hour or so," I said, "and then start calling her friends' parents until you find out where she is. Make sure it's all right if she stays with them overnight and then just wait."

Sure enough, Erin came home the next day. She was sorry, she said. She realized she'd been acting like a spoiled brat and promised to turn over a new leaf.

"Good," her parents said.

"Can I have my stuff back then?" Erin asked. She was very clever, you see.

"No," her parents said, and Erin started into another rage.

A couple of rages and several days later, Erin apologized again. She promised to never, ever be the world's baddest child again.

"Prove it," her parents said. "It will only take a month."

Three months later, Erin finally managed to get her stuff back. When she graduated from her rehabilitation program, her parents told her that the next time she forced them to take her stuff away, she would be required to be good not just for one month, but for three.

I ran into her parents at one of my speaking engagements a few years later. They told me that since being expelled from her personal Garden on that one occasion, Erin had been reasonably tolerable to live with and sometimes even quite enjoyable to live with. She still had her "moments," they said, but nothing that even approximated the horrible-terrible moments she'd had when she was thirteen.

Lowering the boom on a child doesn't always work as quickly as it worked on Erin, but when parents are willing to stand up to a child's hurricane, rehab usually takes no more than six months—the first two or three months of which are no picnic, believe me. Erin was actually a cakewalk compared to some.

Ah, the stories I can tell.

The Bible Tells Me So!

No discipline seems pleasant at the time, but painful. Later on, however, it produces a harvest of righteousness and peace for those who have been trained by it.
—*HEBREWS 12:11, NIV*

The author of Hebrews affirms that discipline must be unpleasant, even painful, to the person being disciplined.

That means that if what parents call discipline is not unpleasant to a misbehaving child, then whatever the parents did, whatever consequence they used, really doesn't qualify as discipline. Earlier in this chapter, I essentially paraphrased Hebrews 12:11 when I said that when children do something bad, they need to feel bad about it. Something "bad" (from the children's point of view) needs to happen in their lives. Sometimes things have gotten to the point where nothing less than really, *really* bad will do. But the author of Hebrews also says that children who have been successfully disciplined reap many benefits: "a harvest of righteousness and peace." You can't get much better than that, but it should be noted that getting from planting to harvesting requires great patience. People with short attention spans are not suited to farming. Furthermore, getting from planting to harvesting is rarely a smooth road. It's usually replete with its share of hazards, crises, and setbacks. So it is with getting from rebellion in children to a state of relative peace and family harmony. Don't undertake such a journey unless you fully understand that. But then, the Bible also tells us that nothing worth attaining is attained without struggle (see Romans 5:3-5; James 1:12).

To Ponder and Discuss

Are you currently dealing or have you dealt in the past with a child who would have benefited from being kicked out of the Garden? Are you or were you reluctant to go to that "extreme"? If so, what were you afraid of? Are or were your fears realistic? Does your child clearly hold the upper hand in the relationship? What would kicking your child out of the Garden consist of?

17

"Snips and Snails . . . and Sugar and Spice . . ."

What are little boys made of?
What are little boys made of?
Snips and snails
And puppy-dog tails,
That's what little boys are made of.
What are little girls made of?
What are little girls made of?
Sugar and spice
And everything nice,
That's what little girls are made of.

—ENGLISH NURSERY RHYME FROM THE EARLY
NINETEENTH CENTURY

A mother had recently attended a conference with her two-year-old son's preschool teacher and was talking to me about some of the teacher's concerns.

"His teacher says he's on the low end of the attentiveness spectrum and on the high end of the activity spectrum," she said.

When did we begin talking like this about little children, as if each of them is a psychological case study? This teacher is using pseudointellectual terms like "attentiveness spectrum" and "activity spectrum," which she probably picked up at a continuing education seminar. And she's "concerned," which is the word this latest generation of preschool and elementary teachers use to demonstrate how much they care.

"And?" I asked.

"And she said it's too early to tell, but he may have ADHD."

Oh my. Her child is a toddler, and this mom is already scared half to death that something may be wrong with him. Furthermore, the something in question has no legitimate scientific or medical status. Cancer, pneumonia, heart palpitations, and hangnails can be seen either with the naked eye or high-tech devices like MRIs, and precisely measured. Their existence can be proved. No such proof exists concerning the pseudomedical diagnosis of ADHD. Furthermore, if such proof did exist, then ADHD would be a legitimate, verifiable medical condition, and preschool teachers would not be able to claim the ability to diagnose it.

The problem is that preschool and early elementary teachers are essentially being programmed during their academic studies to make mountains out of molehills and trained in the art of mumbo jumbo.

"So," I asked this mom, "how many ends of the attentiveness spectrum are there?"

"How many ends?"

"Yes, how many ends. Your son's teacher says he's on the low end of the attentiveness spectrum. So there's a low end and a high end, right?"

"Uh, I guess."

I took a piece of paper, drew a horizontal line across it, and wrote "Attentiveness Spectrum" above the line. Then I marked the approximate midpoint of the line and wrote "Low" under the left side and "High" under the right side. I turned the paper around so the mother could see it.

"It sounds to me like what the teacher is talking about can be represented this way. Do you agree?"

"Yes."

I then erased the word "Low" and replaced it with "Boys." Likewise, "High" became "Girls." I let mom stare at it for a few seconds. She looked up at me and said, "I think I see your point. My son's a boy, and boys are less attentive than girls."

"On average, that is precisely correct. The fact that your son is on the low end of some theoretical attentiveness spectrum means he's a boy. And if you turn this diagram around and retitle it 'Activity Spectrum,' the fact that your son is at the high end means, again, he's a boy. Voilà! We've confirmed his gender. Good news, eh?"

Mom broke out laughing.

Had this mom sought her grandmother's advice concerning her rambunctious, easily distracted two-year-old son, when rambunctiousness and distractibility are at their peak, Grandma would have probably and simply said, "He's just a boy." That was the long and short of Grandma's diagnostic genius. Had the child in question been a girl whose teacher had described her as being on the low end of the "Activity Spectrum" (i.e., being reluctant to climb monkey bars, shying away from playing dodgeball, displaying anxiety at swinging in more than a short, low arc), Grandma would have laughed at the teacher's "concern," saying, "Land sakes. She's just a girl!"

Likes to poke at snakes: boy. Runs away screaming at the sight of snakes: girl. Climbs and walks on the top of the playground wall: boy. Cries at the mere thought of being on a high place: girl. Loud: boy. Quiet: girl. Doesn't seem to care if he pleases the teacher or not: boy. Seeks teacher's approval: girl. Difficulty with sitting still for tasks like coloring within lines: boy. Enjoys and takes great care with fine motor activities such as coloring within lines: girl. Climbs trees even when told not to climb trees: boy. Compliant with instructions from adult authority figures (and wouldn't even think of climbing trees anyway): girl. And so on. It would seem that modern teacher training programs do not teach that girls and boys are different. Maybe that's not a politically correct thing to be teaching—an inconvenient fact. Nonetheless, it's an immutable truth, one that Grandma reminded young parents of as often as she could.

Over the past several decades, psychologists have made being a boy into a quasidisease. Get a copy of the latest iteration of the *Diagnostic and Statistical Manual*—the so-called psychiatric bible—and peruse the criteria for ADHD and oppositional defiant disorder. What you will find are descriptions of behaviors that are far, far more typical of boys than girls. No longer are boys "just boys"; they are now walking disorders. They are inattentive, easily distracted, highly active, loud, impulsive, and often seem to be off in their own little worlds. The "just boys" of Grandma's day needed a firm hand along with the occasional spanking. Today's "concerns" need medication, and psychologists and psychiatrists have conspired to cut out of whole cloth the spurious notion—not supported by any consistent body of research—that these "wrong" boys will need to take medication for the rest of their lives, even though there's no compelling evidence proving that ADHD medications work better than a combination of a healthy diet, regular exercise, and at least eight hours of sound sleep each night. And when they do "work," the word must be put in quotation marks because they often turn rambunctious boys into quiet zombies.

Grandma's take on boys and girls was more on target, by a long shot, than the position on boys adopted by America's schools and mental health professionals. Loud, active girls who "get into everything" as toddlers and, later, like to climb trees are called "tomboys." Loud, active boys who "get into everything" as toddlers and, later, like to climb trees are diagnosed and medicated. One has to wonder whether this is a logical extension of the demonization of traditional masculinity that began in the late 1960s. In any case, today's boys are being held to a standard of behavior that is incompatible with their nature, a nature that is being further suppressed by video games and other electronic devices.

The Bible Tells Me So!

God created man in His own image; in the image of God He created him; male and female He created them.

—*GENESIS 1:27*

From the very beginning, God created humanity in two genders, male and female, and he created them distinct, with different burdens and expectations. While it is true that there are variations in how boys and girls act, in general boys and girls have different temperaments that reveal themselves early and require different approaches in how they are reared. It has become fashionable today to pretend that there are no differences between male and female, but even our overtreatment of ADHD and other "disorders" in boys betrays that there are differences between the two. Grandma believed the truer notion that boys and girls behave differently, and there was no sense in trying to make one group act more like the other.

To Ponder and Discuss

What differences do you see between your sons' and daughters' behavior? Have you been fretting over problems in your children that can be linked to their genders? How can you rear your children in such a way that honors their God-given gender while making clear your expectations?

18

"If All Your Friends Jumped Off a Cliff, Would You Follow Them?"

"No! I would not! But my friends aren't going to do that anyway!" That was my exasperated reply whenever one of my parents asked me their most exasperating question: "If all your friends jumped off a cliff, would you follow them?"

I'm told that variations on this included "If all your friends ran into a burning building . . ." and "If all your friends went into the surf during a hurricane . . ." The creative possibilities are limitless, actually. Jumped into shark-infested water, played Russian roulette, ate poisonous berries, stuck sharp objects in their eyeballs, drank hydrochloric acid, rolled around in poison ivy—you get the idea.

Grandma understood the temptations of peer pressure. She

knew how impressionable children are and how eager they are to please peers who are more popular and especially who appear cool or "with-it." She wanted to share her wisdom with her children, but she also knew that there were things her children would not understand until they were adults and that the more she talked, the more likely it was that her children's ears would fill with potatoes (see chapter 7). So she often employed pithy, if obscure, aphorisms to get her point across.

Child: Can I go to the mall tonight?

Mother: What, pray tell, is your purpose for going to the mall? You have no money.

Child: Just to, you know, like, uh, hang out.

Mother: Like, uh, hang out of what?

Child: No, Mom! That's just an expression. I mean just be there.

Mother: No.

Child: But all my friends are going to be there tonight!

Mother: Here's another expression: If all your friends jumped off a cliff, would you jump too?

Child: But I'm not talking about jumping off a cliff, Mom! I'm talking about going to the mall. That's all.

Mother: No.

Child: But why?

Mother: Here's yet another expression: Because I said so, that's why.

Child: But that's not fair!

Mother: Life's not fair.

When Grandma asked her children if they would follow their friends off a cliff, she was referring to them doing something that would compromise their character or their morals (or something that, for whatever arbitrary reason, she simply didn't feel like giving them permission to do) just because their friends were doing it. She wanted them to stop and think. Unfortunately, because foolishness is bound up in the heart of a child (see Proverbs 22:15) and that foolishness often expresses itself in the form of impulsive, impetuous decisions, Grandma's rhetorical question about friends jumping off a cliff didn't cause her children to think. It caused them to be frustrated, which is why the question was always accompanied with a firm "no."

Grandma's children wanted to be accepted by their peers, and to children, being accepted means doing whatever their peers do. It wasn't that Grandma didn't want her children to be well liked; it's that she knew being well liked sometimes comes with a price. It's fine to be popular, as long as a person does not compromise his or her morals in the process. Likewise, it's fine to be not so popular if achieving popularity would require compromising a person's morals.

When Amy entered junior high school, she looked two to three years younger than most of her female peers. That was a blessing to me, of course, but from Amy's perspective, it was a curse. She frequently—at least once a week—came home from school complaining that the other girls didn't want her around, that she had no friends, and so on. Willie and I felt for her, but we also knew there was nothing we could do to solve her social problems. We could not magically cause her to look more mature. (And besides, having been a testosterone-driven teenage boy once, I did not *want* her to look more mature.)

We listened to her complaints, talked to her about her problems (none of which she had brought on herself), said that things in her life at that moment weren't fair, agreed that many of her female peers were self-centered and mean, and held her when she cried. Nothing changed, of course. She continued to be Miss Unpopularity.

Finally, at somewhat of a loss, I decided to share a different perspective with her. One day, after a litany of complaints, I said, "Well, Amy, I know you're going to have difficulty understanding this, but being unpopular isn't such a bad thing, really."

"How so?" she asked, her eyes full of tears.

"Well, it's teaching you to not need other people's approval to be who you are, to be more independent, to stand on your own two feet."

"Yeah, Daddy, but it hurts!"

"I know it hurts right now, when you're thirteen, but it's going to be a blessing to you someday."

"Yeah, maybe, but it hurts right now!"

From that point on, whenever she brought up the subject of her lack of popularity, I would listen, agree, and then remind her that being unpopular was helping her learn to be less needy of approval, and so on. And she would tell me that it hurt right now. And around and around these conversations went, seemingly going nowhere.

In high school, Amy began to look more and more her age, developed a circle of close friends (one of whom is her best friend to this day), and became a happy camper. One day many years later, when she was in her midthirties and happily married with three children, Amy and I were talking, and she suddenly, rather out of the blue, said, "Daddy, do you remember when I was in junior high school, and I would complain to you about having no friends, and you would tell me it was making me a stronger person? Well, I really hated that. I thought you just didn't understand the problems I was having. But you were right after all. That experience really did make me into a person who is less dependent on other people's approval."

Sometimes it takes years for a lesson to sink in. And there are times, too, when something that doesn't seem good at the moment is good in the long run.

The Bible Tells Me So!

Whoever walks with the wise becomes wise,
but the companion of fools will suffer harm.
—*PROVERBS 13:20, ESV*

My son, if sinners entice you, do not consent.
—PROVERBS 1:10

Do not be deceived: "Bad company ruins good morals."
—1 CORINTHIANS 15:33, ESV

The snares of peer pressure are as old as the hills. Christians armor themselves against peer pressure by reminding themselves that their lives belong to God, not to others, and that their ultimate home is in heaven and not on this earth.

To Ponder and Discuss

As a child, how susceptible were you to peer pressure? Did your parents try to help you resist it? Were they successful? Do you think you can be any more successful when it comes to your own children? If so, how? Is peer pressure something you still have issues with? Do you sometimes allow your children to do what you really don't want them to do, because you feel pressure from other parents? What are some ways you see your children dealing with peer pressure, and how might you want to change your approach in helping them to successfully resist it?

19
"I'm Going to Let You Stew in Your Own Juices"

Stewing in your own juices is similar to lying in a bed you make (see chapter 3), but it's different enough to justify giving it a separate chapter. Both of these antiquated yet perpetually relevant aphorisms refer to children taking complete responsibility for the consequences of their behavior, choices, or undesirable events in their lives, even undesirable events they had little, if any, control over.

The "juices" part of this aphorism refers to the emotions children work up because of some adverse happening. For example, they become very upset because

- when all of their friends can go to a concert, their own parents forbid it.

- they fail to win the spelling bee because they were given an especially difficult word to spell, much more difficult (everyone agrees) than any of the words the other contestants were required to spell.
- their grandparents give them a new bicycle for their birthday, but it is not the bicycle they wanted.
- their teacher punishes them for something they did not do.

When children complain about what has happened to them, their parents listen and might even attempt to sympathize and console, but eventually they simply say, "We're going to let you stew in your own juices about this." They realize, in other words, that the children in question cannot be consoled, that they have manufactured a soap opera out of the situation, one in which they play the starring role as Victim of the Year, so the parents decide to stop talking and simply let the children deal with their emotions without their help. After all, the parents have already tried to help and have failed miserably. The children would rather be victims than accept that life isn't fair and get on with it.

Children are drama queens, and that applies to both genders. They exaggerate the significance of negative events because they love playing the victim. For this reason, I sometimes refer to children as "drama factories" or "soap opera factories." It is precisely when children begin churning out dramas or soap operas that they are manufacturing a surfeit of emotional "juice." That is when Grandma would tell her children that they were going to have to stew in said juice themselves. She was not going to be drawn into their drama. They needed, at that moment, to accept that life wasn't fair. Furthermore, Grandma was not going to try to make it fair for them.

Under similar circumstances, parents today might say something along the lines of "You need to get over it and move on." I like "You're going to have to stew in your own juices" better. It's more poetic.

The reader will remember that in chapter 3, I pointed out that today's parents have a peculiar willingness to lie in the beds their children make. The same is true of stewing in one's own juices. More often than not, today's parents stew in their children's juices. This very odd form of masochism (psychologists call it "enabling") involves parents who become very upset at something that has happened to their children and strive to solve the problem on the children's behalf.

"Well, John," a reader asks, "are there not times when that's appropriate?"

Good question, to which the answer is yes. If something of a dire or life-changing nature happens to children—something they did nothing to bring on themselves—and the children's parents can mitigate the consequences of the event, they should. But the problem with what I just said is that parents who habitually stew in their children's juices are unable to discriminate between dire, life-altering events and the everyday slings and arrows of outrageous fortune. When parents of that enabling sort read the first sentence of this paragraph, their reaction is almost surely going to be "See!

I did the right thing! John Rosemond says so!" Parents of this sort have a great deal of difficulty being even the slightest bit objective about their children. They feel what their children feel, which is the definition of codependency. As a result, they end up solving not just potentially life-altering problems for their kids but also mundane, everyday, trivial sorts of problems that children need to come to grips with. Those problems are lifelong. The earlier a person accepts their occurrence and develops appropriate coping skills— a sense of humor, for example—the better. That person will be happier and will deal with life's never-ending adversities better. That person will probably even live longer. That's why parents need to let children stew in their own juices. Not always, mind you, but a good amount.

The Bible Tells Me So!

We are afflicted in every way, but not crushed; perplexed, but not driven to despair; persecuted, but not forsaken; struck down, but not destroyed.

—2 CORINTHIANS 4:8-9, ESV

I know how to be brought low, and I know how to abound. In any and every circumstance, I have learned the secret of facing plenty and hunger, abundance and need. I can do all things through him who strengthens me.

—PHILIPPIANS 4:12-13, ESV

From beginning to end, the Bible is full of stories of adversity and of people either overcoming or not overcoming it: Moses, David, Shadrach, Meshach, Abednego, Daniel, all of Jesus' disciples, Paul—and that's the short list! The Bible not only tells us that adversity is part and parcel of the human condition and that no amount of money or prestige can prevent it, but it also tells us how to overcome or, at the very least, deal successfully with adversity—through courage, perseverance, and above all else faith in God through his Son Jesus Christ.

During the writing of this book, I began obsessing about a certain situation. It was important to me that the situation result in a certain outcome, but if it had not, my life would not have been ruined or even significantly damaged. Nonetheless, I began obsessing. I began keeping myself awake at night. My wife eventually noticed something was wrong and asked me about it, and I told her about my self-imposed burden. She said, "You need to give that to the Lord, and then you need to trust in him."

Bingo! Willie's simple, straight-to-the-point and right-on-target words snapped me out of it. She could have said, "I'm going to let you stew in your own juices about this." In effect, she did. She was certainly not going to obsess or agonize with me, and she made that perfectly clear. But she also pointed me in the right direction.

Paul says that when he was a child, he thought like a child but that when he became a man, he put his childish ways behind him (see 1 Corinthians 13:11). When children are dealing with some adversity, disappointment, or problem, parents can and should point them in the right direction. They should give good counsel. They can even tell their children to put their trust in the Lord. The problem, however, is that children have foolishness *bound* in their hearts. That's what the Bible says about them in Proverbs 22:15. They over-dramatize adversity, disappointment, and so on. So all the good counsel in the world is likely to fall on deaf ears when those ears belong to a child. The only lasting cure for childhood, after all, is adulthood—and only a valid adulthood of the type Paul refers to, an adulthood in which childish ways have been consciously laid aside.

In the 1970s, actor Orson Welles appeared in television commercials for Paul Masson wine, promising "no wine before its time." In some ways, children are like wine. It takes a long time, requiring much patience on the part of their parents, for them to mature to the point when they are finally capable of laying aside childish ways and taking on the responsibilities of adulthood. I frequently tell parents that it is impossible to talk a child into being an adult. To borrow from Orson Welles, "no mind before its time."

To Ponder and Discuss

Can you identify situations when you should have let your children stew in their own juices? Are you better able, having read this chapter, to understand that by not solving certain problems for them, you can and will strengthen them and guarantee them a more satisfactory life to come?

20

"I'm Going to Nip It in the Bud"

I said in the introduction that present-day parenting is all but devoid of the sorts of sayings that I cover in this book, but "all but" is the operative term. There are two that deserve mention:

1. "Don't sweat the small stuff," which really isn't a parenting aphorism per se. It's applied in a broad range of contexts—the workplace, social relationships, financial matters, and so on—always meaning that one should give more consideration to the big picture than to details. Don't concern yourself with how your child holds a spoon, for

example. It's more important that you teach him or her not to slurp food off it.

2. "Choose your battles carefully," meaning that a parent should not micromanage children's behavior. Deciding which misbehavior, problem, or issue to deal with is strategic. Parents can waste a lot of disciplinary time and energy on matters that are actually of secondary importance. This saying is sometimes used in place of "don't sweat the small stuff" because their meanings are obviously intertwined.

I agree in principle with both of these ideas—or the bigger idea they both represent. But these expressions are, or can be, somewhat misleading. For example, concerning "don't sweat the small stuff," the fact of the matter is that with very rare exception, big stuff begins as small stuff. Blatant, belligerent disobedience might begin with children ignoring their parents when they give instructions. Full-blown tantrums in public places might begin with brief periods of crying. A five-year-old's attempts to hurt his two-year-old sister might begin with not letting her touch his toys.

"Choose your battles carefully" leaves unanswered the question as to which battles are important enough to warrant parents' attention. Where's the line between significant and insignificant? One parent may think it's really no big deal that her three-year-old often acts as if he doesn't hear her when she speaks to him. She believes that sort of behavior is typical of kids this age and that it will pass in due time, so she doesn't assign it much weight. Another mother, however, doesn't tolerate it when her three-year-old ignores her. When it happens, she immediately puts him in time out for ten minutes. She's determined to prevent misbehavior snowballs from rolling downhill.

The mother who gets my seal of approval is the one who doesn't tolerate her three-year-old acting like he doesn't hear her when she's speaking to him. She would also get Grandma's approval because one of Grandma's favorite bits of parenting advice to young parents was "nip it in the bud." The optimal time for a parent to deal authoritatively with misbehavior is when it first appears. Before the proverbial snowball can make one full rotation, children should hear from their parents a clear message to this effect: "I am not going to allow (tolerate, stand for, put up with, accept) talking back to me, and to emphasize my point, I've decided that you are going to spend the rest of the day in a comfortable chair in the living room and go to bed immediately after supper."

Comparing misbehavior to a snowball is apt because, as Grandma knew, small misbehaviors can rapidly become big misbehaviors. A snowball becomes an avalanche, a drip becomes a deluge, a bud becomes a bloodflower. Don't let the snowball make one full turn. Fix the drip immediately. Nip the bud before it can flower.

Parents who don't nip misbehavior in the bud usually end up feeling overwhelmed by it. They excuse one misbehavior, then overlook another, then rationalize another ("He's only a toddler"), and pretty soon they're dealing with children who, in a relatively short period of time, have gone from being fairly easy to deal with to becoming what I call misbehavior machine guns. To mix my metaphors, the children's parents feel like the plate spinners who used to appear regularly on *The Ed Sullivan Show*. They are frantically trying to maintain a semblance of order, but the more frantic they become, the more things deteriorate.

Nipping misbehavior in the bud is a proactive, as opposed to reactive, approach to discipline. Whatever the context, proactivity is defined as anticipating a potential problem and dealing with it before it becomes a reality. That sort of approach to children's misbehavior virtually guarantees that parents will be able to keep their balance in the face of discipline problems. And by the way, it matters less what specific consequence parents use in response to misbehavior than that parents maintain their cool, that the children in question see right away that the parents are unflappable. Giving time outs, taking away privileges, sending children to bed early, canceling a sleepover, having children write sentences—they are equally effective consequences, but only if parents are completely composed. The minute children see they can "get to" their parents (or teachers or any other authority figures, for that matter), it's "Katy, bar the door." All it takes is for one cow to escape through a break in the fence for all the cattle to quickly follow. So make sure the fence is mended before the second cow can get through.

People who aren't proactive are reactive, and reactive

people, no matter the context, are being driven by their emotions. Their thinking is clouded. It is accurate, in fact, to say they aren't thinking straight. If that sounds like you, then choose one misbehavior, develop a discipline plan, and focus on that one problem until it's solved. Then, pick a second misbehavior and do the same. You're obviously already overwhelmed, and you will continue to feel and act overwhelmed if you continue to try to solve all of your children's misbehavior at once. (For more on this strategic approach to discipline, I recommend my book *The Well-Behaved Child*.)

The Bible Tells Me So!

Preparing your minds for action, and being sober-minded, set your hope fully on the grace that will be brought to you at the revelation of Jesus Christ.
—1 PETER 1:13, ESV

You also must be ready, because the Son of Man will come at an hour when you do not expect him.
—MATTHEW 24:44, NIV

The Bible tells Christians to be proactive, to prepare for Christ's second coming, to not be caught with their proverbial pants down when he comes to gather up his church. The importance of being proactive, of planning ahead and thinking with one's head instead of with one's heart, cannot be stressed enough. That applies to all things, but it is particularly applicable to the issue of a child's proper discipline.

To Ponder and Discuss

Do you frequently feel frazzled, overwhelmed, or at wit's end concerning your child's behavior? Do you now realize that this is due, in great measure, to letting misbehavior "snowballs" start rolling downhill, to not acting proactively to nip misbehavior in the bud? If your answer to those questions is yes, then it's time for you to begin taking a thoughtful, organized approach to your child's discipline. Don't wait! Get started! You can do this!

21

"Ask Them No Questions, and They'll Tell You No Lies"

The parents of a five-year-old girl told me she had developed a "bad habit" of lying and asked my advice.

"Tell me about this lying," I asked.

"Well," the child's mother began, "we will know that she's done something, like eating a cookie without permission, and when we confront her, she denies it."

"What do you mean by 'confront'?"

Dad jumped in. "We ask her if she's eaten a cookie," he said, as if I were being a bit thick.

I chuckled and said, "That's the problem, right there. You're asking her a question when you already know the answer. She ate a cookie. You *know* she ate a cookie. Why are you asking her?"

"To give her a chance to tell the truth," Dad said. I sensed he felt I was asking unnecessary questions, in which case, he was wrong. He and his wife were the ones asking the unnecessary questions of their daughter.

"And instead of telling the truth, she's lying," I said. "She says she didn't eat the cookie."

"Right! Every single time. It's infuriating, for one thing, but we're also very concerned. I mean, are some people programmed to lie or something?"

"You might say that children are programmed to lie when they're asked questions, yes. You're familiar with Genesis chapter three, aren't you? The story of Adam and Eve's transgression?"

They looked at one another, then Mom answered, "Yes."

"Then you will remember that when God sees that both of them are trying to hide something, he *asks* them if they ate from the tree of the knowledge of good and evil, and they both deny responsibility. Adam blames Eve, and Eve blames the serpent."

They exchanged glances again, then Dad said, "Yes, we know the story."

"We can all agree, can't we, that God being God, he already knew they'd eaten from the tree, right?"

They answered yes in unison this time.

"Then the question becomes: Why did he ask? That's one for the theologians, but certainly one of the lessons of the story is that when you ask a child a 'did you?' question when you already know she did, you're almost certain to get a lie.

Your grandmother put it this way: 'Ask them no questions, and they'll tell you no lies.'"

They looked at one another again, and then Dad said, "So, what you're saying is that if we don't ask, she won't lie?"

"Not really," I answered. "I'm saying that by asking, you all but guarantee that she's *going* to lie. If you make a statement instead of asking a question, you greatly lower the likelihood that she will lie, but you don't completely eliminate it. If you know she's done something wrong, then don't ask a question."

"What *should* we do then?" Dad asked.

"Make a statement, such as 'You ate a cookie without permission.' And then, before she can say anything, assign a consequence, as in 'so you're going to have to go to bed immediately after supper tonight.'"

Dad smiled. "That's all well and good," he said, "but what if she denies doing it even though we make a statement?"

"Don't let her take control of the exchange," I said. "That's what her lies do. She lies, and you engage in a cat-and-mouse game with her, and that puts her squarely in control. If you make a statement like 'We know you ate a cookie without permission' and she denies it, stay on course. Say, 'We know you ate a cookie, so you're going to bed immediately after supper.' Don't let her lead you down a rabbit hole."

"Will that stop her from lying?" Mom asked.

"Not right away," I said. "But if you stay the course, if you stop asking questions, then yes, she will stop lying . . . eventually."

Grandma had an intuitive knowledge of children. I'm convinced she understood them better than 99.999 percent of psychologists do for the simple reason that psychologists have been trained to view children through the dark and distorting lens of psychological and developmental theory. Having been so trained, and then having recovered from that training, I absolutely know that most contemporary psychological theory concerning children is woefully inadequate to truly understand them.

The Bible gives a clear picture of children. It tells us that a child's nature, which is the same for all children, inclines toward sin, toward doing the wrong, self-serving thing in nearly all situations. "Foolishness is bound up in the heart of a child"—so says Proverbs 22:15. It's not a pretty picture. And the child's heart is not just tinged with a bit of foolishness, as if it's a dash of salt in an otherwise pure nature; rather, it is *bound* in a child's heart. That's an impressive image. It conveys the sense that this foolishness is a primary aspect of a child's nature and, furthermore, that it's a very stubborn, strong-willed trait. Dislodging this foolishness and driving it away from the child requires, therefore, some powerful and steadfast discipline.

One aspect of this foolishness is the inclination to lie. In other words, children are liars by nature. That's another of the lessons of Genesis 3. In Genesis 2, God bestows upon Adam the power of speech and allows him to name the animals (the first act of "dominion" over other creatures). And then, less than five hundred words later, the first man and first woman use the precious gift of language to lie, to deny responsibility for their transgression.

The idea that children are liars by nature bothers some people. They try, therefore, to rationalize or excuse it by claiming that very young children don't realize they're lying—that when toddlers tell what seems to be a lie, they're just using language incorrectly, and innocently so. That's a very romantic notion and, I dare say, naive. In most cases, the children in question are already very adept at using language. If someone were to ask them, "Are you wearing shoes?" they would answer correctly. The same is true with their response to any question that is nonthreatening, as in the following examples: "Did you go to the park today?" "Did you go for a ride in Daddy's car today?" "Are you a boy?" "Do you have a fire truck?" Typical children, by age two at the latest, are answering those sorts of questions correctly. But when asked "Did you take and eat a cookie?"—something their parents have told them not to do—they lie.

This lying is to be taken seriously, for sure, but at the same time it's important that parents not overreact, because if children see their parents make a big deal of something they did, they're that much more likely to do it again . . . and again and again. That's how molehills become mountains.

That's what happened with the little girl in the above story. Her parents made two mistakes: first, they asked questions when they should have made statements; second, they overreacted to their daughter's lies. They made a big deal out of them.

"But lying is a big deal, John!" a reader might exclaim.

I agree, but the paradox is this: if you *make* a big deal out of a child's lying—I'm referring here to the emotion behind your reaction to the lie—the child's lies will get bigger and bigger, and the child will lie more and more frequently.

We should take a lesson from the previous chapter. The best way to prevent children's lies from becoming a problem is to act properly when they first begin to experiment with lying—to nip it in the bud. In most cases, that's going to occur right around their second birthday.

First, ask them no questions. If you know a child has done something wrong, tell, don't ask. If you know a child snuck an illegal cookie, say, "You took a cookie." If the child still denies it, simply stay the course. Do not let the child control the exchange!

Second, immediately inform the child of the consequence of the misdeed. In this case, the entire sequence would be (possibly): "You took a cookie. I've told you to ask me if you want a cookie. You have to sit in time out for ten minutes. Come with me." Make it short 'n' sweet (see the next chapter). Don't belabor the point by going on and on. Keep your cool. Don't make a big deal out of the situation by reacting emotionally.

The parents of the little girl in the above story didn't do any of that, which is why the child's lies had become, by age five, such a big deal. Make a big deal of something a child does, and you are sure to get exactly that—a big deal.

The Bible Tells Me So!

There are six things that the LORD hates . . .
[including] a lying tongue . . . [and] a false
witness who breathes out lies.

—PROVERBS 6:16-17, 19, ESV

If you "flip" the Ten Commandments (see Exodus 20; Deuteronomy 5) from negative to positive statements—for example, from "Don't do such-and-such" to "Human beings are inclined toward doing such-and-such"—the result is a perfect picture of human nature. We are idolatrous, covetous, adulterous, violent . . . and we are, by nature, self-serving liars. All children, therefore, lie. At first, their lies are experimental. They are just another means of testing the waters, of seeing what they can get away with. If they discover they can lie successfully, they continue to lie and get better and better at it. If they discover they can't get away with lying, they stop (some more quickly than others). Adults who lie are people who discovered as children that they could get away with it. There is great likelihood that when they did something wrong, their parents asked questions and in so doing allowed the children to lead them down the proverbial rabbit hole. Because there's a thrill that accompanies getting away with a lie, children can rapidly become lie addicts. It doesn't take long for this to happen, which is why it is so important that parents observe Grandma's wise advice: when you know that your child has done something wrong, don't ask questions. Make statements, and stick to your guns.

To Ponder and Discuss

Have you ever given your children the benefit of the doubt concerning misbehavior only to later discover that they did what they oh-so-sincerely told you they didn't do? All parents want to think the best of their children, but that tendency can sometimes blind parents to developing problems. Can you see yourself in that statement? If your children have already developed a problem with lying, what can you begin doing today to start your children down the path of honesty?

22
"I'm Going to Keep This Short 'n' Sweet"

Typically, Grandma's communications with her children were straight to the point. She was not one to use any more words than necessary. "I'm going to keep this short 'n' sweet" was one of her favorite sayings, reflecting, as did all of her parenting aphorisms, her uncomplicated, straightforward style.

Grandma's approach to raising children was nonintellectual. It did not matter how smart she might have been; she felt that child rearing was a commonsense process, one that God had equipped human beings to do, and no less so than eagles, whales, and bears.

One of Grandma's short 'n' sweets was "no." When she

was not inclined to grant permission to do or purchase some-thing for one of her children, she said no, and usually noth-ing more. If one of her kids asked "Why?" or "Why not?" Grandma answered with "Because I said so"—which the reader will remember was another of her favorite short 'n' sweets. And that was that.

It's quite obvious that today's parents have misplaced Grandma's short 'n' sweet principle, because when it comes to communicating with their kids, they seem to think the more words the better. To cite what is undoubtedly the most glaring example of this wordiness, today's parents rarely say simply "no." They may think they're saying no, but no is not one hundred and thirty-five words; it is only one.

Likewise, they rarely say "Because I said so." They explain themselves, with the intention of persuading their kids to agree with them. This, as we've already learned, is why so many of today's parents describe their kids as argumentative. Explanations, because they sound persuasive as opposed to authoritative, cause children to believe that if they push back, their parents will give in. And they are frequently correct in that assessment.

Grandma used the fewest words possible for two reasons:

1. The more words one uses, the less authoritative one sounds, and successful discipline is mostly a matter of presentation. If one looks and sounds like an authority figure, children are much more likely to listen and do as they are told.

2. Children's ears shut down after the thirteenth word, and their brains shut down after the twenty-seventh word. Those are my estimates, based on years of personal and professional experience. One would think those numbers would increase as children get older, but that's not at all the case. As many parents can attest, teenagers' ears and brains shut down even earlier.

Children have not changed since Grandma's day, and Grandma's ways still work. Try them and see for yourself.

The Bible Tells Me So!

When you pray, do not keep on babbling like pagans, for they think they will be heard because of their many words.
—MATTHEW 6:7, NIV

Interestingly enough, God is not impressed by verbosity, and neither are children. If you want to get your point across to God, use the fewest words possible. Brevity of speech is characteristic of humble prayer, and God loves humility. Likewise, if you want to get your point across to a child, use the fewest words possible. Do not prattle on. Be short and sweet. The likelihood that children will accept your decision is inversely proportionate to the amount of words you use to convey the decision. "No" sounds authoritative. "Honey,

I wish it were possible for me to give you permission to do that, but it's really not. Mommy just feels that's not a very good thing for a person your age to do, and yes, I know your friends' parents are giving permission, but I'm just concerned something bad might happen, and if it did and Mommy wasn't there, Mommy would feel terrible, and I can't be there because I have a garden club meeting, and I'm responsible for the speaker, and I just can't let the girls down, so the answer is no, but I love you!"—does not sound authoritative at all. It sounds whiny, wimpy, and wishy washy. "No" is one word. "Honey, I wish . . ." is one hundred words.

To Ponder and Discuss

When you talk to your children, and especially when you talk about "issues," do you tend to go on and on and on, often repeating yourself, thinking that the more you say, the more likely it is they will hear you? Do you now understand that the fewer words you use, especially when you talk about "issues," the more likely it is that the kids will not only hear you but take you seriously? The solution to your loquaciousness disorder is to plan ahead for "issues-oriented" conversations with your kids. Decide what you're going to say in advance of saying it. Whittle your presentation down so that it's sharp and to the point. Do you see the difference?

23
"You're Too Smart for Your Own Good"

This chapter is dedicated to my pastor, Dr. Scott Gleason, at Tabernacle Baptist Church, New Bern, North Carolina, because of his sermon on January 11, 2015, during which my ears perked up when he began talking about Proverbs 3:7 ("Do not be wise in your own eyes . . ."), because I've been there, done that, and still occasionally (too often) catch myself doing so.

"What in the world does he mean by that?" I would silently ask myself whenever my stepfather, shaking his head, would tell me I was too smart for my own good. It seemed contradictory. How can being really smart be a bad thing?

He meant, of course, that I was smart enough to think I

could fool people. He was right, of course, like he was right about most things. I not only *thought* I was capable of fooling people, I *did* fool people. But the person I fooled most was me.

For the first forty or so years of my life, I thought I was self-sufficient. I convinced myself I could do without God, for example. That's the foremost example, in fact. I believed that people who needed a god in their lives, a god who told them what to do and not to do, were weak. I was not like them. I was strong both intellectually and emotionally. I didn't need some mythical, supernatural being to hold my hand while I went about the business of living the good, successful life. I was making lots of money, lots and lots of parents seemed to hang on my every word, and people often treated me like I was a celebrity of sorts. I had a better-than-average marriage and better-than-average kids. What more could a guy want? One might say my life's theme song was "My Way." I was Mr. Independent.

Then, in the early 1990s, I began reading articles and books on intelligent design and creationism—books by credible scientists and philosophers like Hugh Ross, Gerald L. Schroeder, Phillip E. Johnson, and Michael J. Behe. I've always considered myself an intellectually honest person—defined as a person who, when shown evidence that contradicts a currently held belief, will change his or her mind—and to make a long story short, I changed my mind. Newly convinced that Darwinism was a theory without credible evidence, I began to believe in the Old Testament Creator God. But I still couldn't wrap my head around that "Jesus thing." Walking on water? C'mon! He must've been walking on a hidden sandbar. Bringing people back from death? No way! They weren't really dead; their biological processes had simply slowed down a lot. Rising from the dead less than forty-eight hours after a horrific scourging and crucifixion and appearing, fully healed, to his disciples after walking through a solid wall? Give me a break! I was *way* too smart to believe in that mumbo jumbo.

In 2000, Mr. Independent Smarty Pants was in a bookstore looking for a book on the historical Jesus—something that would continue to feed my need to believe that I did not need a Savior, that I could figure things out on my own—and the Holy Spirit led me to Lee Strobel's *The Case for Christ*. Quite to my surprise, Strobel's book opened the door, and Jesus walked boldly into my life. "Are you ready," he asked, "to give up your childish fantasies of self-sufficiency, to stop making a fool of yourself, and to admit that I'm real and you need me more than you've ever needed anything?" At that moment, I stopped believing in the almighty Me and gave my life and my work to him. It took fifty-three years for me to come to my senses, but nothing happens, I now know, according to anyone's time but God's. I also know, now, that my stepfather—an atheist—was spot on about me. I was too smart for my own good. But then—and I say this with absolutely no satisfaction—it took one to know one, as they say.

The Bible Tells Me So!

It is written: "I will destroy the wisdom of the wise, and bring to nothing the understanding of the prudent." Where is the wise? Where is the scribe? Where is the disputer of this age? Has not God made foolish the wisdom of this world?

—*1 CORINTHIANS 1:19-20*

There are a number of people in the Bible who are too smart for their own good. The Pharisees come immediately to mind. In the Gospels, these scholars of the law are depicted as trying again and again to either confound Jesus with a legal problem or trap him into giving a wrong answer to one of their clever questions. And every time they do so, Jesus demonstrates to them and whatever witnesses are present that they aren't nearly, by a long shot, as smart as they think they are. For sure, they're "smart" concerning the law. They can probably quote Leviticus word for word, but their legalism has actually made them blind to God's truth as revealed in his Son. They can't see past the ends of their own turned-up, legalistic noses, which only goes to show that there's a huge difference between possessing a lot of information and being in possession of true wisdom.

Grandma, the protagonist of this book, is a good example of that difference. She might not have had more than an eighth-grade education, but where children were concerned, she possessed more wisdom than one hundred psychologists. The Pharisees were blinded by the law. They were so convinced that salvation was obtained through adherence to the minutiae of the law that they were unable to see that Jesus was its fulfillment. As Grandma would have put it, they couldn't see the forest—the big picture of God's plan for salvation—for the trees. When it comes to children, psychologists are blinded by theory. Psychologists know theory—Grandma simply knows children.

To Ponder and Discuss

In what ways are your children too smart for their own good? Do they believe they possess superior traits that are going to bring them sure success? If you answered yes, are you willing to accept that there's nothing you can do to dislodge those beliefs from their underdeveloped heads? That your children's free will is stronger than your wisdom? Are you ready, then, to relax and let their lives take their inevitable courses? Are you ready to stop trying to correct everything about them that you think needs correction? Are you ready to accept that only an encounter with God the Son is going to straighten out some of the kinks in their thinking and behavior? If so, make a list of those things and simply pray that they experience an encounter with Jesus sooner rather than later. Then, wad up the list and toss it out of your life. In other words, stop thinking you are your children's personal Savior.

24
"Give 'em an Inch, and They'll Want a Mile"

"But Dad!" a child exclaims. "You let me ride my bike to the movies last week! The mall is only a few blocks farther!"

Another child wants to know why his parents won't buy him the latest gadget. After all, he reminds them, they bought him the last gadget he wanted, and this one is no more expensive.

A teenager whose parents recently allowed her a certain privilege has an outburst because her parents refuse to allow her latest request. "Why not?" she demands. "This is no different from that!"

And on and on it goes, proving the truth of one of Grandma's favorite parenting sayings: "Give 'em an inch, and they'll want a mile." Children are rarely satisfied with the status quo. They want more, more, and even more, and then some. Concerning privilege, they think they are more capable than they actually are. The other side of that equation, however, is that parents are generally inclined to believe that their kids are less capable than they actually are—responsible parents, that is. So children who can only handle an inch want a mile, but it's equally the case that their parents are only willing to give a half inch. That's the story of the parent-child relationship. It's the story of growing up. The child is straining at the end of the leash while the parents are pulling back with equal or greater force. The child takes two steps forward; the parents pull the child one step back.

The fact that children who are given an inch want a mile only speaks to the fact that they want to grow up as quickly as they can. That's not a bad thing. After all, the earlier children successfully emancipate, the better for all concerned. So children push limits. And the more successful at moving a limit, the harder they push. The problem is that children don't have a realistic grasp of their own limitations. They tend to overestimate their capabilities, which is why children break a lot more bones than adults do. As a consequence of their general lack of caution, they tend—and of course this is more true of boys than of girls, of snips than of spice—to unwittingly put themselves in harm's way. That's one reason God made parents, to protect children from themselves (and other people and things as well).

This is a fact: the more parents give in, the harder children will push the parents to give in. That is simply another way of saying that if you give children an inch, they will want a mile.

This is also a fact: being too rigid, too draconian, about rules and limits is just as problematic as being a pushover. In other words, defining limits is not just a matter of saying no. It's also a matter of changing no to yes at the appropriate time. For example, it's appropriate to tell a six-year-old that she can't walk one mile home from school, but it's also appropriate to tell a twelve-year-old that she can, under certain circumstances, walk the mile from school to home. At around age twelve, you want to change that no to a qualified yes.

Parents who are too rigid, who say no almost as a reflex and long past when it's appropriate, are likely to cause their children to adopt deceptive means of getting what they want (and maybe even should have). Or they grow children who, the first time they experience any freedom, run wild. They've been pent up for so long behind their parents' barricades that when the barricades are no longer there—when they go off to college, for instance—their pent-up yearning for freedom bursts forth in the form of disorderly, random, and even self-destructive conduct. We've all heard stories of kids who go off to college, completely lose it, and flunk out within a year. Many of these kids never experienced any reasonable amount of freedom before college. After eighteen years of living in a very comfortable cage, but a cage nonetheless, they go stark raving mad as soon as the cage door is opened.

So, indeed, it's important to enforce limits and to not give in to children's badgering, to their near-constant attempts to wear you down to the point where you throw up your arms and say, "All right then! Enough! I'm tired of fighting with you! Go ahead!" It's important, sometimes, that you not give an inch. But it's also important that when the time comes, you give the inch. Or maybe even a foot, or a yard, or ten yards. You probably don't want to go from an inch to more than a foot at any one time, though.

Children develop self-discipline, which includes good impulse control, from parents who are able to find that balance.

The Bible Tells Me So!

You shall not covet your neighbor's house. You
shall not covet your neighbor's wife, or his
manservant or maidservant, his ox or donkey,
or anything that belongs to your neighbor.
—*EXODUS 20:17, NIV*

The Ten Commandments constitute the limits God places on our behavior or, more accurately, the limits he wants us to place on our behavior. The law set forth in Leviticus was for the Israelites, to set them apart as God's chosen people; the Ten Commandments are for us all. As I've already pointed out, they are a "negative" description of our sinful nature. "You shall not covet" is God telling us that we need to recognize the covetous impulse in our nature and learn to control it. The same is true of all of the other nine commands. Children need limits, but so do we all.

To Ponder and Discuss

Have you been guilty of giving in to pleading, badgering, and the like from your kids and letting them do things you really didn't want to let them do? What causes you to give in? Are you tired of fighting? Are you afraid that if you don't give in they won't like you? Identify why you give in and then determine how you're going to deal with them the next time they try to get you to give an inch . . . and then a mile. Be proactive! Think it through! Develop your resolve before the next episode of badgering begins!

Conclusion
Oh, and One More Thing...

As I've been writing this book, I've been telling people about it, mostly in response to the frequent question, "What's your next book going to be about, John?" When I tell them that it's a book explaining the meaning, contemporary relevance, and biblical connections of twenty or so of the more popular parenting sayings of the 1950s, a good number of folks have asked if I'm going to include "If you don't stop crying, I'm going to give you something to cry about."

Indeed, that was something some 1950s parents said to their kids, when said kids were upset about something of no lasting importance, if the something in question was even important at all. My stepfather used to say it to me when I was crying about something insignificant. Maybe some other kid had taken my baseball and thrown it over the fence, and I'd been unable to find it. He meant that if I didn't stop crying, he would give me a spanking. That was just plain mean, wasn't it? Yes, but I've long since forgiven my stepfather for his occasional meanness and tried my best to put it into proper perspective.

Grandma's generation endured great hardship. They grew up during the most difficult economy this country has ever suffered. It was so bad and lasted so long it earned the name "Great Depression." And then, before the Great Depression had abated, World War II hit like a sledgehammer. During these years of trial and tribulation, my mother's family was evicted from their ancestral home in the Lowcountry of South Carolina. Along with her three younger siblings, she spent the next seven years of her childhood in an orphanage because her mother, a single parent, could not afford to feed, clothe, or house them. My stepfather's parents, both European immigrants, emancipated him at age sixteen because they could no longer afford to support him. He went into the army at seventeen, fought in the Pacific theater in World War II, and then went to college on the GI Bill while working at hard-labor jobs to pay living expenses.

My mother's and stepfather's stories are par for the course for their generation. They lived hard lives until the war was over and recovery began. My point is that the phrase "If you don't stop crying, I'll give you something to cry about," as mean as it was, is understandable. It's forgivable; at least I've forgiven my stepfather for it.

Furthermore, from all I gather, that particular saying was not in common use in the 1950s. It was an anomaly, used by people who had themselves been scarred by life. So, no, I chose not to include it in this book. I included those that I felt are still relevant meaningwise and that are biblically supportable. "If you don't stop crying . . . " is definitely not a reflection of God's plan for the family. Not by a long shot.

I hope you have enjoyed reading this book as much as I enjoyed writing it. I hope it has inspired you to begin incorporating Grandma's parenting wisdom and point of view into your child-rearing practices. If so, I absolutely know you won't regret it.

About the Author

John Kirk Rosemond was born in Asheville, North Carolina, on November 25, 1947. He spent his first seven years in Charleston, South Carolina, during most of which his mother was a single parent. Upon her remarriage in 1954, the family moved to the suburbs of Chicago, where John graduated from Proviso West High School in 1965.

John earned both his undergraduate and graduate degrees in psychology from Western Illinois University, where he was also elected to the Phi Kappa Phi national honor society. In 1999, his alma mater conferred upon John the Distinguished Alumni Award, which included the honor of giving WIU's commencement address.

Since 1971, John has worked with families, children, and parents in the field of family psychology.

John and Willie were married in 1968. They lived in west-central Illinois until 1974, when they moved with their two children, Eric and Amy, to North Carolina. Today John and Willie live in an 1855 house in the downtown historic district of New Bern, North Carolina. "The next time we move," John says, "God will be the moving company."

John and Willie are committed believers in the eternal lordship of Jesus Christ. They attend Tabernacle Baptist Church in New Bern, where they grow weekly through the sermons of Dr. Scott Gleason.

In 1976, John began writing a weekly parenting column for the Gastonia, North Carolina, *Gazette*. In 1978, the column was picked up by *The Charlotte Observer*. In 1979, it was syndicated nationally. Today John's column, which appears in more than two hundred newspapers, has the distinction of being the longest-running syndicated column written continuously by a single author.

John's first book, *Six-Point Plan for Raising Happy, Healthy Children*, was published in 1989. It has sold more than 400,000 copies to date, and his books (now totaling twenty, including new, completely revised editions), cumulatively, have sold well over a million copies.

Presently, his time is devoted to speaking and writing. John is one of America's busiest and most popular speakers. He's known for his sound advice, humor, and easy, relaxed, engaging style.

Over the years, John has appeared on numerous national television programs including *20/20*, *Good Morning America*, *The View*, *TODAY Show*, *Later Today*, CNN, and Bill O'Reilly, as well as numerous print and radio interviews.

More information about John is available through his two websites at www.johnrosemond.com and www.parentguru.com.

All his professional accomplishments aside, John is quick to point out that his real qualifications are that he's been married to the same woman for forty-seven years, is the father of two responsible adults, and the grandfather of seven well-mannered grandchildren.

PARENTING
BY THE BOOK
(sold individually and as a group study)

───────── ❦ ─────────

John Rosemond is available for
speaking engagements throughout
the year. Consult his calendar,
shop his bookstore, and more at
WWW.JOHNROSEMOND.COM

John's membership website:
WWW.PARENTGURU.COM